NINETY NINE NAMES

NINETY NINE NAMES

A collection of short stories by

VINCENT JEWELL

Angustus Publishing

Copyright © 2022 by Vincent Jewell

All rights reserved. No part of this book may be reproduced in any manner whatsoever without written permission except in the case of brief quotations embodied in critical articles and reviews.

First Printing, 2022

For Anna

Introduction

Elie Wiesel said "God made man because he loves stories." Each of us are custodians of a vast array of these stories. In some stories we are the characters, either the main protagonist or simply onlookers, whereas some are tales that have been shared with us by others. Together, they form a complex tapestry that informs and interprets the thing we call "our lives."

In this collection, Vincent Jewell is inviting us into thirty-seven of his life's stories. They are not comprehensive stories, more vignettes, mere snapshots of various moments in people's lives.

For the most part, the characters have no names and are completely unidentifiable. But those of us who were present when these events were born, can recognise them and recognise ourselves even though they have been generalised, fictionalised and abstracted. At one level, they simply depict an event or a circumstance, but through these vignettes, a deeper meaning is glimpsed. Events that seem mundane are infused with a transcendence that challenges us to look again at our daily lives and appreciate the ineffable mystery that lurks beneath.

I consider it a great privilege to be publishing this anthology and cannot recommend these stories highly enough.

Darren Koch
Seaview Victoria 2022

Contents

Dedication		v
1	The Buddha Woman	1
2	The Zen Architect	6
3	The Elephant Watcher	11
4	The Infidel	18
5	The Sparrow Assassin	25
6	The Chosen Apprentice	32
7	The Monk in Exile	38
8	The New Evangelist	44
9	Gink	49
10	The Antipodean Pilgrim	55
11	The Bad Mother	61
12	The Forward Scout	68
13	The Chess Players	73
14	The Grey Nomad	78
15	The Boxer	83

16	The Rainbow Man	89
17	The Young Surfer	96
18	The Fire Fighter	102
19	The Naga Babba	108
20	The Moon Boy	112
21	The Soldier's Son	117
22	The Control Freak	122
23	The Unlikely Missionaries	128
24	The Hairy Hand	135
25	The Lone Camper	142
26	The Militant Devotees	149
27	The Armchair Revolutionary	155
28	The Auschwitz Survivor	160
29	The Mzungu	165
30	The Scruffy Bodhisattva	171
31	The Dislocated Dreamer	177
32	The Only Adult	182
33	The Retired God Botherer	188
34	The Kindergarten Teacher	195
35	The Child Killer	200
36	The Surprise Guru	207
37	The Recalcitrant Priest	212

Author's Note	223
About The Author	226

I

The Buddha Woman

The Buddha woman had no use for small talk or for charity. She was beyond that now. Silence was all the currency she needed ever since the fall. Not even noon day devils or midday hustlers chasing deadlines would make her turn her gaze. Not now the world was on fire. Not while pity was consumed by avarice. Not while the lengths of God went begging for attention.

She was invisible until the stray pilgrim saw her sitting still like Buddha at the hottest time of the day. A small patch of shade was all the mercy she sought. There she had spread her grimy blanket and her begging bowl. There she sat open eyed, falling and falling into the marrow of silence. There she was taking the leap deep down into the soul of the world one breath at a time.

One breath was all she needed to feel the fragile extent of things. In one breath she held all things passing. All the woe and all the joy, all ten thousand times ten thousand of it, each life time at a time. One breath was all she needed to keep witness.

It was only a stray pilgrim that noticed her. He had not travelled much but he had an eye for resistance when he saw it. It was her seditious lack of industrial purpose that caught his eye. Then in a single glance her cloak of invisibility lifted. She did not blink and neither did he. Suddenly they had time to waste.

He had seen the thick smoke harrying the shrouded pedestrians. He noticed how the gulls did weary spirals in the funereal breeze, surfing smoky thermals in the burnt glow of an admonishing sun. He could smell death thick and close in the air. Up and down, and back and across, the country was on fire. He could feel something keening in the heat, the smell of agony and tipping points.

Uninvited he sat down on the hot pavement beside her.

"How did you get here?" He asked without preamble.

The Buddha woman looked neither left nor right. She kept her silence. She had shed her old life like a snake sheds its skin. Some traces of a past life flashed back from before the fall, before the accident. She was too poor now to pay rent to her haunted past. She had become empty the hard way. Words were a luxury she could no longer afford.

The stray pilgrim figured silence spoke louder than words and settled down to becoming invisible. They were a colony of the forgotten, human detritus defying the indifferent dust. Side by side they sat in the soiled street looking at the world from the bottom up. The silence stretched. Mostly they were unnoticed except for a flickering glance of judgment or a momentary flash of pity. The day wore on and then out of the blue a passer-by announced to the ruined air:

"You know, the funny thing about all my good times is that they always seem to disappear."

The stray pilgrim could not help laughing out loud. Someone tossed a coin that arced and hit him in the face and then got trampled underfoot. Only the gulls knew where it went. The Buddha woman did not move. She kept her vigil, eyes wide open, catching hold of the world one face at a time until the stray pilgrim asked, "What are you doing here?"

The Buddha woman had nothing she wanted to say. She turned and fixed the stray pilgrim with a look of recognition. How could she tell him his face contained the map of the world? She could see it in every line and lineament. How could she tell him there was only one degree of separation from all things arising? How could she say how hard it was to do precisely nothing? How could she tell him the only way into the spiralling never ending mystery of things was down not up? How could she tell him how ambushed by impossible grief she had been? How once she used to have a name. Once, her world had been safe and dependable, bland and boring before she had crashed and fallen.

Her old life was a fading memory now. Once she had been a daughter, a mother, a wife, a tax payer and lawful citizen. Once neither her vices nor virtues had been spectacular. Just like everybody passing by she had spent her time running for the future or looking back to the past. Her life had been mundane, manageable and pedestrian. She liked sex, chased success and wanted entertainment. She had drank a little too much and watched too much television. She had turned up for working bees and given to charities that came door knocking. She had gone to church once a year on sufferance and preferred life unexamined, until the sky fell in.

The accident was her fault. Running a red light under the influence and getting T boned towards the next world. The other driver was hurt and so was she. Her son did not survive. The magistrate threw the book. Her husband divorced her and meth became her lover. She shrivelled up inside and wanted death delivered hard and slow. By the time she got parole she had a hard habit if not a satisfying one. The first time she shot up she got a backwards glimpse of nirvana. Every other dose barely numbed her pain.

Then one day the sky had really fallen in, hard and blue and unannounced. One minute she was standing and the next she was face down in the street. Her whole world became single pointed. There was a light calling her, getting closer. There was a silence dissolving everything. She de-molecularised, becoming one with the endless blue. Suddenly there was absolutely no distance between her and the lengths of God.

Not that she used that name. She never spoke at all. For a few weeks she was in hospital hardly moving and then almost as suddenly she stood again. They sent her to rehab after that. They kept poking and prodding and giving her drugs and tests and then one day she just walked and kept on walking right out under the hard blue sky that now was her teacher. She knew she had only one purpose.

Atonement.

Not sacrifice. She had done that already and failed. She had bled rivers for her own sins and still they floated back to haunt her. But once the sky fell in, she had nothing to defend and nothing to lose. The old order had passed away and now she was at one with everything under the sun. Now there was no distance between her and the present moment. It was all there in the clear still silence. Now, breath by breath, she could breathe in the very soul of the world.

Someone religious might have called it enlightenment but she was not religious. She had no need for spiritual heroics about saving a sinful world. There were saints and *bodhisattvas* for that. Her solidarity with everything was simpler. Bone simple. But she could not tell that to the stray pilgrim. She knew everyone had to work it out for themselves.

The stray pilgrim held her eye for as long as he could before blinking. When he looked again he saw her staring out at the passers-by. He could see they were all harassed with purpose and demand and too irritated by the heat and smoke to look him in the eye. He was still invisible but something told him only the Buddha woman saw that the emperor had no clothes. He was glad of her silence. That she had proffered no answers. He had not travelled much but he could recognise an accident of grace when he saw one. Getting ambushed by love or grief was always on the cards. How could such immensity be met with anything but silence?

He stood up and became visible again. He gave the Buddha woman a knowing smile but she was clear eyed and far away. There was nothing beggarly about her. No hangdog look for succour. No entreaty for solace under a dark sky. Everything she had to say was before her. Written down on cardboard he supposed in her own hand. There it was propped up against her begging bowl.

Witness.

2

The Zen Architect

Every lunch time the architect took a short walk. Every lunch time he found something to marvel at. He always walked slowly with an eye for rapture. A single rose unfolding would render him spell bound. A lone tree was an angel in hiding. A stray leaf on the wind would suspend him in fractal wonder. A solitary stone was a piece of infinity. Every human face was a road map to the face of God. A passing cloud unlocked the sky and brought it gently down upon his head. Even the white noise of passing traffic was a secret mantra inviting him to listen closely. Some days he thought he could almost hear it. The sound of one hand clapping.

Nothing was mundane.

Every lunch time he would invite the great blue dome of sky to fall again. Each time it did he discovered everything belonged. There was no distance between himself and all things arising. The present moment was entirely sufficient. The past and the future were less appealing. He had lived many lives. He had survived Stalin and Hitler. He had been blown along by fierce winds as a son, a conscript, a deserter, a husband, a lover, a charmer, a raconteur, an artist, a designer and a keeper of silence.

He knew his time was almost up. He knew all of life was a stage and he had been lucky enough to have a part in seven acts. Soon it would be stage exit. He had been quite the thespian, speaking six languages, escaping Stalin's minions as they went searching house to house and on the run from total war. He escaped the Germans when they conscripted him into their army. He escaped being AWOL in Austria watching dog fights in the afternoon over cheese and wine. He escaped Marshal Tito's partisans when the Germans re-conscripted him under a false name. He escaped the Americans when they fire bombed his town. He had survived marriage and love affairs and wayward ungrateful children. He survived studying architecture in France and insufferable French superiority. He had survived the Australians with their incivility and ignorance. He had cheated death too often to cheat it much more. He was content. He had seen a lot of death. The future rolled on with its assurance of fatality. The past he preferred to leave to forgotten dreams and shadows. Only rarely did the shadows return.

Most lunch times he took the same route through the park and around the block. He had an architect's eye for elegance and simplicity. He knew every tree by name. He loved lingering near roses and caressing hedges. Every front garden he passed invited fascination. Nothing was dull if you had the eye for it. His Australian grown children tended to disagree. They got bored endlessly. They had grown up fat and entitled. They were beholden to their own superficial times. They were untested by suffering. It wasn't their fault that they belonged to such a coarse and uncivil people. He did not blame them for that. All the same the architect thought boredom was a mortal sin.

The architect was a dapper man who stood out in his bright pink bowtie, white boater hat, red shoes and brightly striped jacket. He firmly believed style and substance belonged together. He adored women. Every lunch time he found more than one goddess to adore. Often he would dip his hat and wink just a little with a deft flourish of his mahogany walking stick. He was too old to be taken seriously or to keep custody of the eyes. Often enough he was rewarded with a sly smile in return. How could any lunch time walk ever be dull when such beauty walked the earth? Life was good. The present all that was needed. Rarely did the shadows return.

The architect had almost learned to forgive himself and put an end to his own civil war. He had let go of slapping his own cheek. He had grown tired of being wound and knife. He had seen enough of executioners, including the vampire in his own heart. He had seen the world broken to pieces and reduced to ash. He had seen enough victims to no longer add himself to the whirlwind. He was careful not to unlock old memories needlessly.

Most lunch times the shadows were lifetimes away. Only rarely did they lay ambush and break through his silence. His love of beauty kept him safe unless some stray signal or event triggered unwanted memory. This lunch time he wasn't so careful. It started with two German tourists walking by. Hearing that language always played tricks. He had not spoken it in years. Just one simple difficult word uprooted him.

"Wie?"

How what? How come just "how"? It was just a word to express curiosity. All she said was "how". The past should have been safely locked away. Today he was unlucky. At the same moment a light aeroplane flew low over the park. The sound of the plane dissolved time. The shock took him completely by surprise. The park and the trees and the tourists and the flowers were all gone. Only the plane chewing through time remained.

He was back in Lithuania on a rainy summer's morning. There

was a young German officer and a Russian prisoner of a war. He was the translator. The men were watching a fleeing Russian army retreat across a river. Suddenly there was a huge explosion. The Russians had blown the bridge! The three men huddled as the blast wave whipped downstream. Chaos replaced order. The Russians had blown the bridge with their men still on it! Where there had been steel and stone there were tanks and trucks and horses and carts and men dangling grotesquely in the ripped air. All the young German officer could say in outraged disbelief was, "Wie? Wie? Wie?"

The officer was a boy man just like himself. Neither of them believed what they could see happening only a kilometre away. Only the Russian did not seem surprised. The Russians had blown the bridge and their army! The blast was huge. The death toll was unimaginable.

The young officer became furious and even more afraid. He kept asking, "How? How? How?"

The architect did what he was told and asked the Russian. All down the years he could not forget the prisoner's words with his fatalistic shrug, "There are so many of us and so few of you."

The officer was aghast and astonished. The world had gone mad. He could see it and so could the architect. The war was lost. They might win battle after battle but no army on earth could stand against such massive disregard for life. Sturdy bridges, steel and concrete, blood and iron would not suffice.

The war was lost.

Not even the impeccably dressed skull and bones SS men with their black uniforms, sharp eyes and Wagnerian conceit would prevail. They had met their match in death dealing. It was his job simply to survive.

The rupture in time shifted. Other shadows lingered in the lunch time light. He went on to be conscripted twice and to desert twice. He took shelter under false names and became a cheese maker in

Austria. He was clever and daring and kept his head down. Even after the Americans had almost killed him, he was there to welcome their tanks and loud speakers playing the Andrews Sisters' boogie.

The architect preferred Mozart to Wagner. The Austrian was on the side of life not death. Too many had died. Countless many. More than the architect and the astonished traumatised German officer could ever imagine. The only protest was to survive.

The small twin engine plane kept moving. He was back free of shadows under a bright sun. Once again he took in all of creation and all its beauty one step and one breath at a time. He looked down at a garden of petunias rioting with colour. They were lighting up the day and renewing all creation. Once again, the whole blue dome of the sky was in his lap. The twin engine plane was just a speck disappearing in the distance.

And, somewhere, underneath it all, just out of earshot, was the sound of one hand clapping.

3

The Elephant Watcher

The scientist was the only person in the room watching the elephant. All the others looked elsewhere. Conspiracies were easier to bear than facts. His children and grandchildren chided him for using the C word. His wife remained industrially cheerful. His list of old friends grew thin. Most of his colleagues and friends now stayed away. One even suggested the cancer might be his fault. His sister even suggested it was because of unresolved resentments and negative emotions. He was blame worthy. Somehow he had invited death into his cells due to low self-esteem and unforgiveness. Her solution lay in turmeric, prune juice and rebalancing all his chakras. The scientist was too polite to argue.

Those friends and colleagues that did visit talked in safe circles. They waltzed around the elephant with news of football, Netflix and the weather. They avoided eye contact and covered their tracks with gossip and complaints about how politicians were doing a drive-by on tertiary education. They talked long and hard about everything except the elephant.

The scientist did not have the same luxury. He had a reputation for academic excellence and rigorous objectivity. His whole life had been about weighing data and sifting evidence. He was good at grasping facts. Now the facts were grasping him.

The oncologist had been direct. "The pain will get worse before the end. When in need don't be too brave."

"What do you mean?" the scientist wanted more information "You haven't got long."

"How long?"

"I don't know, weeks, not months, but it will get rough, so don't be too tough. Your whole body is under siege and bit by bit it is shutting down. All of your senses will be affected, maybe the last will be your hearing."

The scientist appreciated direct answers. He had been logging his own decline with his usual rational thoroughness. The oncologist was right. He was getting thinner inside and out. All his senses were on notice. He took a sip of his coffee and tried not to notice how dull his sense of taste was. It had been like that for weeks now. Every day he felt he was losing something. He was gaunt, reduced and now his vision was going. Only his sense of touch remained obdurately keen. Every day the pain was getting worse. The morphine patch was a reluctant concession. He did not want to lose clarity. He had to keep watch on the elephant. No visitor ever did. He wondered if this visiting priest might be different. How would he go with the elephant? They sipped coffee and talked in run way circles while he grimaced and fought down yet another wave of pain.

It was a bright late winter's morning and the scientist's wife had just bustled in with more coffee and biscuits. The scientist watched the priest thank her politely. His wife rarely stood still. She kept game face on and remained relentlessly cheerful. The scientist wondered if the priest was observant enough to see what he saw behind his wife's armour-plated smile. She too, seldom looked him in the eye but when she did the scientist caught a glimpse of her sheer dismay. It was always just out of reach, but it was there; a barely disguised horror, and a grief, and something approaching unmitigated panic only just covered by a thinly maintained pragmatism.

Both men chatted amiably. They were reminiscing about being children of an analogue age. They were nostalgic for the times before the rise of mega tech empires and the tyranny of social media. They weren't happy about it. The scientist told the priest that his children and grandchildren were now digital natives fully slotted and tangled inside the matrix. They inhabited a brave new social media world where the panopticon eye never slept. Edward Snowdon was right; henceforward no generation would know privacy. They were all at the mercy of a new breed of robber barons reducing heritage and culture to monetized commodity and dopamine rush. They kept it light until the scientist popped the question:

"What is going to happen to me when I die?"

The scientist kept his tone neutral and conversational with one eye on the elephant and the other on the priest.

The priest tried not to choke on his biscuit while avoiding eye contact. A wave of panic washed over him as he blinked in the bright morning light. In all his years of ministry no one had ever been so direct. He tried not to flinch and shiver. He felt naked like an actor without a script. The polite scientist deserved something more than dogma and regurgitated nostrums. Sermonising would not avail. He gripped his coffee tight while his cookie crumbled. His head was racing looking for some formula or script to materialize in the naked morning light. All he had was total panic. The question broadsided him like a torpedo amidships; like he was being weighed in the balance and found wanting. A life spent pontificating would not suffice. The silence stretched on and on.

The scientist wasn't in any hurry. He was used to people not looking him in the eye. He was used to long difficult silences. He figured that like most religious people, the priest was good for theory but light on for evidence.

The silence extended. Eventually the priest admitted:

"I don't know," and stared into his coffee. His head kept racing. Was the scientist asking about dying or the life hereafter? Despite all his prayers and the many funerals neither seemed within his competence to comment on. It took an age to look up at the scientist and stop blinking.

"So have a guess," the scientist couldn't help a chuckle. "You are the spiritual expert that will outlive me."

The priest felt stung. Nothing serious was coming to his rescue so he joked, "Maybe Woody Allen was right when he said, 'I am not afraid of death, I just do not want to be there when it happens.'"

Neither man laughed.

The scientist was in a mood to cut to the chase so he said, "So much for endings, what about beginnings or is death God's mistake?"

The priest couldn't help a nervous laugh. "God has lots of mistakes to answer for. You could fill libraries with evidence for the prosecution."

The scientist nodded. "So it seems. But that is hardly very comforting."

"That's God for you." The priest knew he wasn't making it any easier. "You are a chemist, you know everything transmutes but never ends. It seems each birth is owed a death. But things just change rather than ever end. Death and life are one weave."

"You still haven't answered my question." The scientist leaned forward compelling the priest to make eye contact. "What will be left of me?"

There was another extended silence. The priest tried to loosen his grip on the coffee cup. "I don't know. There is a Zen saying, 'no snow flake ever falls in the wrong place.'"

"Thanks for the riddle. What does it mean? Lots of my grandchildren get called snowflakes these days."

The priest could feel himself sinking. "I think it means God is very good at being particular."

"That's even less comforting." The scientist could feel his reserves of politeness draining away. "So much for God talk. What then? What will happen to me? Do you have any spiritual advice?"

The priest could feel the sting in the air. He gulped some more coffee and forced himself to make eye contact. "I don't know. Maybe all I can say is we all cross the bar and enter the ocean refusing no river. Me, you, everyone. Maybe we are just candles to be extinguished when the sun rises. Maybe we are just salt expanding into water. Maybe all we can do is trust and surrender and let go. I don't know."

"That simple huh" the scientist did not hide his growing frustration.

The priest tried not to flinch. He stared out the window wanting to die and disappear in the late winter light.

"Sorry about the God talk. I have received just enough education so as to become permanently confused. We priests can hide all the day long behind our God talk."

"So, you really don't know do you?" The scientist permitted himself a wry smile, "other than drop everything and let go."

"Pretty much that's it," the priest admitted. "It is very easy to turn God into a cipher for avoiding reality instead of dealing with it."

"At least reality is dependably certain," the scientist chuckled briefly before fighting down another wave of pain.

"Yeah," the priest nodded, "death and taxes, the one universal nonnegotiable."

"Shouldn't you add love to that list?" The scientist allowed himself a little irony. "Isn't that what you experts say God is?"

The sting in the air had become palpable

The priest looked down at his outstretched fingers trying to suppress the panic he felt in his core.

"I'm sorry. Yes, God is love. That really is the only thing we can say definitively."

"Definitive?" The scientist raised his eyebrows just a little.

"I hope so," the priest admittedly lamely. "Nothing else will make sense of our insane world. I guess Jesus is the great sacrament or icon or archetype of love pointing us all towards a light and life and love that doesn't die. He died into that love that never ends. Saying much more than that can get awfully complicated and confusing."

"You guess?" The scientist raised his eyebrows a little more. The priest noticed there was a sharp light in his eyes.

"Yes, I am not a scientist."

There was another long silence. The two men just looked at each other. The priest saw how hollowed out the scientist looked. He wondered if the man saw something he did not. Was the veil parting or was there only dread and terror kept at bay by thin civility? He was sick of feeling such helpless panic so he asked.

"Are you afraid to die?"

The scientist permitted himself a wintry smile.

"Shit yes! Thanks for asking. No one else does." He felt himself almost on the verge of tears.

"Me too," the priest said.

There was another long silence. The scientist decided to grin rather than cry. "Glad you said that. Makes sense. You haven't died yet. I'm scared and lonely and sick of being sick. I might be ready but trouble is, no one ever comes back to say it is all okay."

"Only Jesus they say," the priest knew he sounded lame.

"Prove it!" the scientist managed another pale smile.

"I am afraid I am going to have to outsource that one to a higher power," the priest managed to smile back.

"Then what now?"

The priest looked down at his hands again. The morning light was filling the room. He was all out of answers. "I don't know," he said. "Go with it. Stay with it. Surrender what you can." He knew he wasn't improving on the silence.

The scientist tried to stop shaking. He knew the priest was out of his depth but he appreciated direct answers.

It was then his wife bustled back masked in her cheerful smile. Abruptly their conversation shifted while the scientist watched the elephant return to the corner of the room. The two men went back to discussing the rise and rise of mega tech empires.

The priest excused himself soon afterwards. When he got back to his car he put his head in his hands and groaned out loud. Sure enough, he had not seen the elephant. Not directly at least. Although he knew it was there. He shook his head and cursed his unbelief and pastoral ineptitude.

It was an age before he was able to move.

When he did the elephant was right with him, right on his back, riding all the way home.

4

The Infidel

The chaplain hunched against the biting easterly. It seemed every time he visited the private prison it was there; a diablos wind, running hard against the grain of the world. It made the air feel wrong and hard. No matter how much he braced himself it left him feeling listless and exposed. He knew it really didn't have to do with the weather. Sure, the dry wind raked his face and probed his soul. It was the only thing free to come and go over the high barbed wire fences. It was always on the inside the great dread descended. Just as he was about to press the flesh and do the rounds of the units it tied his guts in knots. Try as he might to keep his game face from slipping, the diabolos wind always made him feel like a boy on a man's errand.

The exposed, treeless prison was made for the devil's wind. Its high wire fences contained a sprawling complex of brutally ugly buildings. Beauty was too expensive. Indifference and something far more brutal than the architecture felt ever present. The chaplain saw it in the bored slouching officers and their sullen stares. He could almost smell it on the wind. It smelt like the burnt end of profiteering out of human misery. None of the prisons the chaplain visited were safe places. Everywhere he went there was a hectic, hidden, fury and danger. Everywhere the system merely paid lip service to rehabilitation.

Once he got past the irritable officers, the chaplain made a valiant effort to keep game face on. It never really worked. After a while spent floundering around the mainstream units, he made his way to the protection unit. The diablos wind stayed with him all the way asking questions. Why was he here? Did he have any faith at all?

The protection unit always felt more hectic and dangerous than mainstream. It was more confined and unfriendly eyes kept keen vigil. The chaplain had a service to conduct. He clutched his bag and his little boom box ghetto blaster and set up in a little room provided for the service. The only attendees were two serious sex offenders. They were pariahs amongst the pariahs. As usual they fawned over him obsequiously and made a show of prim piety. The chaplain tried not to let it stick in his throat. He said the prayers quickly feeling a desperate need to be anywhere else. Outside the easterly keening under the eaves kept asking questions. Who amongst them really had faith? The sex offenders had caved in eyes and opaque smiles. The chaplain felt his game face slipping. He was not up to smiling back. He had too much faith to be an atheist but not enough for something as difficult as an interventionist God. The diablos wind echoed his less than sanguine mind. Was not all religion silly as a wheel? Was not dogma mostly humbug? Why had he wasted his life with a messiah complex? Should he be cool and get with a Buddhist program? Jesus might be as nice as apple pie if you stayed away from the fine print. But whether Jesus was nice or not, an itchy question kept scratching. How was Jesus anything more than just another dead half God like Krishna or Hercules? The diablos wind reminded him he had no idea.

On the way out, some of the Muslim boys wanted a word with him. They jibed and joshed as he passed their unit. They were on to him.

"Hey, padre got any music for us?"

"No, only the divine silence for you guys." He laughed as they gathered around him, smiling through sharp eyes.

"So why do you worship a false God?" one of them cut to the chase as the others circled, smiles narrowing.

"Yes, why do you say three when God is only one?" Another challenged. "Why do you say Jesus is God when he is only a prophet? Three never into one. There is only one God."

"Just as well God doesn't have a religion," the chaplain joked. He was in no mood for an argument.

The Muslim boys all frowned. It sounded very much like infidel humour to them.

"No! Islam God's true religion! Islam a religion of peace!" one of the boys was particularly adamant.

"Is it?" the chaplain thought it best to be a small target.

"Yes!" the adamant boy didn't look as good natured as before. "So why you make Jesus into God when only a man, only a prophet. God only one not three."

"I guess it is complex," The chaplain was all out of answers.

"No! Not complex. Islam a simple religion. God is one and Muhammad is his prophet; peace be upon him." All the boys nodded in agreement.

"Okay. Maybe you boys are right." The chaplain kept smiling. "We Christians have a much more complex religion. Too many strange ideas. Maybe that's why you guys conquered us so easily at the beginning.

"No!" the adamant boy was frowning hard. "Islam a religion of peace. Not conquer. Just final truth for all the world. Only conquer when we are defending ourselves."

"Gosh, is that why you ended up with so much territory?" the chaplain couldn't help having a dig.

The Muslim boys looked at him blankly.

"No! Only way is submission to Allah. God never three, only one. Jesus never God! All other religion false religion."

The chaplain had nothing reasonable left to say so he smiled and waved the Muslim boys goodbye. They waved back through tight smiles, eyes bright with triumph. They knew an infidel when they saw one. They ribbed him a bit more and let him pass.

The chaplain had seen the same melody sung before to other lyrics. Prison had a way of producing armour-plated, born-again believers. Hard places made for hard religion. There were lots of angry young men wanting a severe God. There were lots of damaged men looking for a father or a protector. It made sense to get hard core religion if you thought about it on their terms. The world was full of danger and abuse. Every which way you looked someone was trying to take you down or stand over you. It then made sense to get it right with the biggest stand over man of them all.

The chaplain waved and kept moving. Another prisoner came towards him; the one some of the boys called captain. He was a white-collar offender shunted into protection from the bare-knuckle dangers of mainstream. He was called captain because he had been a head kicker in the corporate world. Some wise cracker had called him a captain of industry. The chaplain hardly knew him. Prison was full of society's bottom dwellers. It was very rare to find someone who had fallen so far from the board room floor. He had fallen from the top of the food chain to the bottom. Once upon a time he used to have minders and minions keeping the swill from the gates. Now he was just a pasty old white man keeping his head down amongst all the muscled tattooed war paint. He was the fat old pig.

The captain liked the status quo the way it was. It was only right the weak were meat and the strong should eat. It was only difficult to find he was the one getting grilled. It was his mistake to not stop whining. Justice had been perverted. The more he complained the further he fell. The panorama of entitlement took some letting go. It was hard to be a loser that any plastic gangster with an attitude could stand over. Nobody liked him, so he made a bee line for the chaplain. It was a relief to find someone as weak and pasty as himself.

"Hey, padre what is justice? What does the Vatican say?"

The chaplain paused. He had often enough asked himself the same question.

"You might need lots of lawyer's guns and money to find out."

"I don't have enough. But I bet the Vatican does. Keep those three monkeys working. See no evil, hear no evil, speak no evil, and keep the black money with the white. Maybe I should have been a priest," the captain complained. "I should have kept close to my friends and made my enemies even closer like they say here."

"Do you have any friends?" the chaplain found he did not like the captain very much.

"Not anymore." The captain tried to make a joke of it. Neither man smiled. "It's a jungle in here," the captain waved at some other prisoners in the yard. "See that big guy over there. Four guys tried to stab him in his cell the other day and he just leant back and stared and said 'only four?' That's what they say at least. He is the war lord here. That's what they say. You know what? He and I are the only ones rich enough to have our kids go to private school. All the same he is as shit scared as I am. He more or less told me. Like he was in a western and any day soon someone is going say 'draw'. There are lots of crew in here ready to go off like booby-traps."

"Yeah, I know him," the chaplain admitted. "He used to be an altar boy."

The captain looked momentarily confused. "You come around here much?"

The chaplain could feel the diablos wind whispering. He could feel his aversion for the captain growing exponentially. "Only when I have to these days. It seems Jesus is on holidays."

The captain eyed the chaplain sharply.

"Lucky fucking you. Point is; you never can be too sure of your place in the food chain. I used to be one hundred floors and more above all of this shit but I got stitched. Got altitude sickness I guess you could say. You talk to me right now, and right now you are on the bottom."

Suddenly the captain just looked pathetic and miserable. The chaplain regretted all his distemper and lack of kindness. He gave the captain a tired smile and his arm a pat.

"Maybe we all can benefit from flying at low altitudes. Just about everyone I meet in this place has been stitched. Lots of perversion of justice along the road."

Just as the chaplain gave the captain a sad smile something flashed through the air in front of them. Both men started, it was only a tennis ball. It had been thrown on purpose.

The officers were off slouching in the far corner of the yard. The chaplain adjusted the boom box and started slowly walking towards the officers. He felt a finger poke his shoulder.

"Hey cunt, I like your box, give it to me."

The chaplain knew it was a case of mistaken identity. His coat was a near prison issue green and his identity tag was hidden. All the same something snapped. Suddenly, Just like that; he was weak meat floundering on the bottom, he was mere prey; easy kill for the strong to eat.

But it was the charged C word that removed his safety switch. There was something about all the malice packed into that one word "cunt!" hearing himself so called made the chaplain want to be real nasty. True he was a chaplain who knew not a few in polite society but he was a working-class boy. He was suddenly enraged by the smell of his own fear. Fight felt like a more satisfying option than flight.

He stopped and looked back at his interlocutor. The prisoner looked scrawny and vicious. He had a sideways sneer that made the chaplain more determined to pause.

He gave the prisoner a smile and then stepped backwards narrowing the distance. He smiled again.

"You can have it," he said, "If you ask me really, really nicely." He stepped back again. He was in striking distance.

"Hey, padre" one of the Muslim boys yelled out, on his feet and all smiles.

The scrawny interlocutor suddenly stepped back burying his expletives. He slunk away in petulant fury. It was the rule. Everyone knew it. Striking a chaplain would bring worlds of pain down on his head.

The Muslim boy gave the chaplain a thumbs up. Allah was merciful and had saved the day.

The infidel was free to go and Allah with him.

They would prevail next time.

5

The Sparrow Assassin

The sparrow assassin had neither mercy nor courage. It was a slaughter in the shearing shed. The cold clear night offered no protection and the divine regard seemed otherwise engaged. The feathered aeronauts were not even given one last hard fall. The assassin and his assistant were on them in a blink. Stunning them in hard white light and drilling them with lead slugs. Life was over in a flash of exploding feathers and blood, no questions asked.

The boy assassins roved over the lanolin waxed floorboards not bothering to be quiet. There was no thrill of the hunt, no careful stalking, only the delight in the kill. The roosting sparrows offered neither flight nor fight as they were extinguished at point blank range. Not even the dull click of the slug gun or the muffled impact of blooded metal on wrought iron was enough to startle them. The ambushing light was severe and deadly. It had only one purpose. To serve the gun.

The boys huddled together in earnest devotion to their weapon. It was an upgrade. A high-powered slug gun with a rifled bore, powerful enough take down rabbits or even a human if fired with expert intent. The sparrows had no chance.

It was the first time the sparrow assassin had killed with a gun after years of make believe. As an urban boy he had grown up playing war games. He loved all his World War Two comics where the bad guys were always marked for defeat. No matter how many times they went all guns blazing and yelled "Achtung!" It was always "Arrrgh!" that had the last word. War was fun and easy. On television guns were power and instant solution. Clint Eastwood rarely missed and neither did Charles Bronson. In the end no matter how much excitement, there was always one bullet left with a villain's name on it.

The sparrow assassin and his cousin spent the summer days roving over the granite hills of the farm playing war games with cap guns. They stalked patiently amongst the noon day shadows mimicking death and demanding surrender. Sometimes they roved together, imagining they were advancing scouts, bravely waiting in ambush for goons and Huns. But make believe was a pale act next to genuine kills. And on the farm there was always something to kill and real big guns to kill with.

Two days earlier in long afternoon shadows the sparrow assassin's uncle had shown him and his father the farms arsenal. There was a slender rifle his uncle dismissed as a 'pea shooter'. There were three shot guns. A single barrel, a double barrel and a five shot pump action blaster that might have given '*The Rifleman*' and his Winchester a run for his money. More deadly than them all was the point 303 calibre rifle with a telescopic sight. The sparrow assassin was not allowed to touch it but his father had been given a go. The weapon had gone off like a huge fire cracker and the sparrow assassin's father's body shook with the force of it. The retort kept echoing off the granite and everyone looked on with something like awe. The grownups spoke in satisfied appreciation about how the

303 could kill a man a mile away and that a mere five hundred yards target would be an easy kill. They held the weapon in turn with a care that might have been religious. And then finally, the sparrow assassin's uncle had brandished the slug gun with its rifled bore. Just a play thing for country boys. He and his cousin couldn't wait to see it in action. They were dismissed and spent the rest of the afternoon targeting beer cans and jam tins.

That same night they went out with the adults spotlighting for rabbits. The boys were not allowed to use any of the shot guns but were given the job of surfing in the back of the ute swinging the spot light. They bumped and bounced slowly across the paddocks with the spotlight bifurcating the dark like the angry eye of God. At first, they saw nothing as they patrolled the perimeter. But then little lights would wink and blink furtively at the edge of the light and then freeze into form. They were no match for the paralysing light. Once exposed the little lights turned into stunned rabbits flinching in industrial glare. The sparrow assassin's uncle never missed. It was pretty hard not to. Only the shot gun blast would jolt the rabbits into motion until going a little further another set of blinking lights would materialize as victims.

They were barely out for half an hour before the sparrow assassin lost count of kills. It was carnage not sport. No one felt at all sorry for the rabbits. They were invaders, pests marked for extermination. The adults were very pleased with themselves and so were the boys. They swung the light with determined care and gave little whoops as the ute followed the trajectory they plotted. Each kill seemed like validation and reward and all the violence no more disturbing than pulling up weeds. The killing spree two nights later in the shearing shed came effortlessly after that. The boys had no feeling for feathered jam tins. They had found an appetite for death and a gun they were willing to serve.

After nearly a dozen kills, the sport wore off for the sparrow assassin. Something inside him twitched and jarred awkwardly. The sparrows were too easy to kill, too meek in death, too innocent. They offered no offence or affront. Something about their sheer passivity unnerved him. Their sweet evening song he took for granted along with their lives. Something inside him began to protest at some as yet unrecognized injustice. He couldn't name it but killing was not quite the fun it was cracked up to be and death, when delivered so emphatically was so disturbingly final. Not a single sparrow was play acting and not one fluttered back to life demanding it was someone else's turn to play dead.

The killing spree came to a halt soon after that and the city boy sparrow assassin never played with his country cousin on the farm again. Back in the suburbs guns were not as visible. Sure enough he talked his father into buying him a slug gun of his own. For a while he played with it constantly, shooting tins. It was not as complete a weapon as his cousin's gun. It didn't have a rifled bore and it sounded an even duller click when fired. But he loved the feel of it cocked against his shoulder and the frisson of power that came when he lined things up in the sight. Sometimes he would wander off the urban grid to unkempt border scrub and let go at bronze winged pigeons in flight. They were harder targets than sparrows. Eventually his delinquency went too far and he was apprehended by the police for taking aim at overhead power lines. The sparrow assassin's father was furious and he never had access to the slug gun again.

A few years later he went on a hunting and fishing expedition with older mates. His only weapon was his fishing rod. The trout were harder to lure but when the time for killing came he felt the old jangling, jarring, twitching in his gut. There was less distance from the kill than with the gunned down sparrows. The wily trout took some seducing but they died in a thrashing orgy, reeled hook first into the asphyxiating air. Their death was too slow, yanked by keen steel into the unfamiliar air to bleed and drown before they had their heads bashed in on the rocks. After the second fish was reeled in, the sparrow assassin lost the taste for it.

His older mates had fewer qualms. They decided to go into the bush with the shot gun. The startled rabbits were too quick. The first kill was a startled red bellied black snake which the shot gun cut clean in half. Then one of the crew startled a wallaby and shot it at point blank range. It was not a quick death. The shocked thing twitched and jerked until the happy hunter shot it dead with a second shot.

They left it there after that. No questions asked. Road kill without a road; all of them indifferent to whether the kill was necessary or justifiable. They forgot about it as they drove home in an old Zephyr at homicidal speed and an exhaust of dirty jokes. The sparrow assassin laughed too but couldn't forget that jerking feeling in his gut. The sight of the bloodied wallaby with its guts blown out kept haunting him. Try as he might to forget there was something about it that reminded him of sparrows exploding in hard light.

City boy killer that he was, he lost interest in guns after that. He still loved playing war games in his head. In the legend playing in his own mind he was still killing villains and paying homage to the gun. He preferred Clint Eastward or Bruce Willis on the big screen. It felt safer to keep violence vicariously contained to the movies. In the movies violence felt justified and right. It was just pretend, unlike the cruelty and carnage rending the real world.

The sparrow assassin took a while growing up. Along the way he caught sight of more than one death and rending. There were other days when the sparrows came back to haunt him. Once it was a wombat he ran over late at night. Another time a snake he ran over flat out on a hot road. There were road kill magpies and other wild things destroyed in the wake of his passing. As he got older he saw just how many other living things were terminated by his passing.

The older he got the more he saw. Just turning on the lights or starting the car made him implicate in the death of many small and tender creatures. He could feel some sort of reckoning coming. Getting out of bed and drawing breath was no longer an innocent act.

Some things he killed with little qualm. Mosquitoes, blowflies, certain spiders, European wasps, ticks and sand-flies. But like a lot of other soft city killers, he had learnt how to keep nature at a distance and live inside a fortress of artificiality. Nature felt more manageable behind glass and well-defined edges. There was less chance of being disturbed except by unwanted visitors like rodents, ants, cockroaches and spiders.

One night one such unwanted rodent got caught in a steel spring trap the sparrow assassin had set in the name of keeping things clean. The sparrow assassin was woken by the snap and squeal and clamour. He went to the laundry and found the rat maimed and convulsing as it swung about in its trap. Again, he felt that familiar jerking dismay in his gut. Being too squeamish to kill with his own hands he went for the garden rake and lent on the rat's neck with all his weight. It took what seemed like an age to die.

It was nothing but a rat, a pest, an urban nuisance coming to an end. No one at all would remark upon it. But as the assassin lent with all his weight on the rat's neck, he felt the rat's staggering will to live. It ran all the way up the rake and into his hands. The sparrow assassin felt every twitch and tremor of resistance. It seemed to him that life itself was confronting his murderous hands. It was there in every violent convulsion confronting him with an unspeakable vitality and will to endure.

Shaken, the sparrow assassin did the deed. He looked at the fallen rat and sighed. It is just nature he thought to himself; just the red-toothed claw of it.

"Everybody is guaranteed at least one really bad day." he said to the fallen rat. He went disconsolately to bed. Somewhere in his dreams he heard sparrows singing and voices whispering.

"You too, you too."

6

The Chosen Apprentice

Life's a bitch and then you die....

The hip hop rant came for the apprentice right in the middle of peak hour gridlock. She made a lunge for the kill button on the car radio but it was too late. The rapid beat and delivery breached her defences. It wasn't her kind of music but she was already nodding and tapping grimly. The rant was close to her bones. The rappers were not short on conviction. They sang like they had the scars to prove it but were light on for answers. Despite herself the apprentice kept on tapping. Her fingers were the only things moving in the traffic. The rappers were telling her to get high or die. It might have been sage advice. She had tried getting high often enough but the rappers neglected to say what goes up must come down. And, then, life went on until it didn't. The apprentice tried to keep her impatient fingers from dancing. It was too late. It wasn't the first time a song she hated stuck like super glue in her mind all the day long.

The peak hour grid lock was going nowhere. Life after lockdowns was going nowhere. She was on the road to nowhere. Why, oh why, did she take so long to reach the kill button? The air around her felt stir crazy. The machine had awoken requiring sacrifice. Cabin fever had given way to road rage. Business was trying so hard to be usual but something terrible was amiss. It felt like lots of quiet desperation was on the loose. The strain of a long lockdown was a bitch. People were frayed, exposed, lonely, anxious, unsure, tired, stressed and wanting someone to blame. Even walled away from the other commuters behind glass and metal she could feel it. Business was a long way off from being usual. It felt like she was in a caravan of hungry ghosts.

The apprentice tried to shake herself out of it. The traffic was insane. She was getting cross. Where did all these people come from? Why weren't they carpooling and reducing their carbon footprint? Surely they could get by with zoom or take public transport. Surely they didn't all need to be there! She tried in vain not to curse. So much for bloody home-schooling! So much for an enlightened post COVID work life balance. The machine had awoken and wanted to go driving. Cabin fevered zombies were at large, getting in the road of real working people like herself. She had a hammer with lots of nails to hit. She was busy! Let the paper shufflers and digital natives in zoom-land stay home! Life may or may not be a bitch but gridlocks were every time.

The apprentice couldn't shake off the song. She had her own scars with a thing or two to prove. For so long she had been treading water, almost drowning, never waving. Ever since her sister's death it had lurked beneath the surface. Life was a bitch alright. Grief and loss had riven her family. Ever since ground zero, depression and anxiety had pushed her down.

Her big sister was the star of the family; a one woman tour de force, a sunny faced avatar that some unkind God had chosen to do slowly on the rack of cancer. There was nothing her avatar sister could not have achieved. She was brilliant, good looking, sensitive, gregarious, adventurous and passionate for life. No one had been more intense and more playful. Everyone liked her unless they got her sharp side which the apprentice knew was the lot of all the little sisters in this world.

Her big sister was both an artist and scientist, a party animal and eco revolutionary. No one else the apprentice knew had ever seized her days with so much serious passion. Growing up in her shadow was not without difficulty. The bar was set high. The apprentice was whip smart herself but laziness was her secret rebellion against the world. It was her way to protect herself. Watching her sister slowly get hollowed out made her inclined not to do what she was told. Her not so quiet rage came easily after that.

No one in the apprentice's family was left intact after ground zero. The impact zone did them all in different ways. The apprentice went raging and loathing at the world. Her mum became an atheist and went very, very quiet. Her father divorced her mother and was intent on suing God for damages. He refused to become an atheist and kept looking for miracles no matter how bad he felt. Despite never having the slightest inclination to go to church; God and the end of the world was nearly all he spoke about.

The apprentice did not particularly care if God existed, except to provide an apology for upending the lot of them with unbearable grief. Just surviving day to day was enough strain on her faith. Partying hard was better than tortured conjectures about the deity. She went to uni but wasted as much time as she could. Study just made her bored and restless. Sex and drugs were frequently disappointing. She deferred and went flogging real estate but only when she laid down her pen for a hammer did she start to come back to the surface. Three years later she was getting to live not just survive. Life was not a bitch! No! Not always. Making things with her hands felt so much better than writing politically correct essays about post structuralist queer theory. Sure enough, academia was a bitch. Getting stuck in the traffic and surviving corona time was a mere slap in the face with a feather after that.

To a point.

Gridlock could do strange things to a girl. Waiting and patience were not a part of her lexicon. The intrusive rappers got consigned to history but her fingers still tapped furiously. She pulled her rear vision mirror towards her to get a better view of what was behind. The carpark snaked out of sight in both directions. She resumed her cursing. What was wrong with the world?

The apprentice was warming up for another burst of expletives when she heard the siren sounding in the distance. So that was it! Somewhere there was an accident. She hunched down in her seat resigned to going nowhere. She looked in the rear mirror and could see an ambulance with lights and siren sounding alarm as it snaked alongside the parked cars in the emergency lane. Out of the blue she was seized with a sort of panic. One medical emergency conjured another. She hated hospitals and avoided doctors. The sound of the siren was the sound of distress and pain and death. Suddenly she was having difficulty breathing. The ambulance was almost beside her and all she wanted to do was find somewhere quiet and sit until the panic passed her by.

As soon as the ambulance passed she pulled over to the emergency lane and killed the engine. There was a tightness in her chest that felt like she was breaking in two. She hunched down further and tried to breathe. Just as suddenly she was flooded with a great tide of peace that felt like it was rising up and filling every part of her. She started crying but no longer felt sad. Something indelible gripped her heart. She knew for sure she was not alone. In every direction a great peace seemed to be flowing over all the world, over all the grief, over all the COVID, over all the cabin fevered zombies and most of all; all over her. She wept openly, unseen by the gridlocked world. Some immense intimacy had drawn close and somehow, she knew she would never be quite the same again. Now she was called and summoned. It did not make sense but that bastard of a God who did not exist had to be behind it. A great embrace had fallen upon her and a great intimation. A voiceless voice spoke secrets to her soul. She was loved and called and she would suffer both weal and woe. She was no longer her own property.

Minutes and an age later she rang her father.

"Hey, Dad, I don't know what's just happened. It's weird, real weird, but I feel God has just reached out to me." She babbled on in her excitement telling her father how God had recognized all her pain.

"What else did God do?" The apprentice could hear her father's cranky sceptical tone. Very quickly the peace felt like it was ebbing away. She felt annoyed. She expected her father to be more pleased, more understanding.

"Geez, Dad, I don't know. You are the one who keeps on saying God talks straight with crooked lines. I just felt something or someone amazing recognize all the pain I've ever had. It was like a divine apology."

"Hmmph!" she heard her father snort. "And what else did God have to say for himself?"

The apprentice felt she could hear her father cogitating. She was getting cross. Why wasn't he excited like she was?

"Bloody hell, Dad! I don't know. Like you say the world is burning. I guess God was saying get prepared to do something. It will be hard; it will be scary but I am with you."

There was an uncomfortable silence on the other end of the phone. She heard her father mumble, "Well at least he *apologised*."

The apprentice resisted the urge to snap back. "Thanks, Dad. Now's not the time. Love ya."

In the distance the apprentice could see the ambulance lights still flashing. The world was turning again. She started the engine and snuck back into the line of traffic.

She was called and she was summoned.

She was not on her own.

7

The Monk in Exile

As soon as the monk in exile hit the water he knew it was a bad idea. Killing himself was a lot more difficult than he thought. It wasn't the grand sweeping end he imagined. Instead of sinking, like he planned, he swam. The life instinct was a kicker. His will to live came as a surprise. He had been in India too long. Long enough to forget that unlike the locals he could actually swim. The Ganges did not want his foreign body. His grommet days spent surfing and weathering long Australian summers came back to mock him. Fortunately no locals saw him jump.

For a kilometre or two he tried drowning not waving. It was no use. Adrenalin took over. His black hole of despair was no match for the brown water of life. Holy Mother Ganges had other plans. His desperation was unworthy of her mercy but she dumped him ashore a mile or so downstream anyway. She would not allow him to disappear like some renowned '*sadhus*' sometimes did. He had a long way to go before some greater grace carried him across the yawning chasm of birth and death.

No one saw him drag his muddied saffron robed body up the bank. He threw a backhanded prayer at the river. "Thanks for nothing."

The hot Bengali sun was already evaporating the evidence of his folly. It hammered down on his shaved head with hurtful intent. He went looking for a bit of shade and sat down. He allowed himself a bitter smile. He no longer believed in death and rebirth. He shook his head and laughed out loud at his heresy. He no longer believed in Mother Ganges. He no longer believed at all.

Years of asceticism had drained his vitality. Almost without knowing it the monk in exile's faith had all but evaporated like a shrinking water hole drying after the monsoon rains had gone. Like rising saline; first his agnosticism and then his atheism had finally reached the surface stripping away the old greenery of belief. The slow melt of disillusionment had done its part. There were sex and money scandals in the monastery. A bit like the Vatican but downsized. There was the stress of monastic duties. There was the attrition of a meagre red rice and spicy vegetables diet. A diet that stripped his guts, broke his teeth, and left him ulcerated and thin

But most of all he was lonely. Bone lonely; living under an acquired name in an acquired life that no longer made sense. Try as he might his recalcitrant heresies could no longer be swept under the orthodox carpet. Nothing was certain anymore except death and uncertainty. Even believing in unbelieving was too much of a stretch.

The monk in exile rose to his feet and straightened out his '*dhoti.*' No one was the wiser to his reckless act. No one would ask questions. Only God had a clue and he did't exist anyway. And if he did who cared? He started walking. The sun grew more hurtful. The monastery wasn't far but just a few steps later he narrowly avoided stepping on the head of a king cobra. Fortunately the thick serpent was too hot to be bothered with him. He gave a bit of a yelp and hopped clear.

"Better luck next time," He gave the snake the finger and some free encouragement.

The shock of another adrenaline shot snapped him out of his distemper and dragged up recent trauma. It was just a fortnight since armed bandits had attacked the village compound. An old man had been hacked to death with machetes. Some others had been severely wounded and some young girls raped. During it all some of the villagers ran to the monastery. In all the commotion and pandemonium the monks had all gone running down the road on a moonless night. The monk in exile had too. On the track he remembered seeing deeper shadows sliding away. He was sure he missed more than one cobra in all the panic. He could still hear the sound of keening and furious weeping. They were all beside themselves with rage and fear. They all knew the bandits would be back again.

Sure enough they attacked the big compound the Hare Krishna's lived in just two nights later. The bandits were not expecting to be met with an M 16 machine gun. He could hear the machine gun fire in the distance. The bandits were turning the delta into a war zone.

Later one of the bandits was heard groaning for hours outside the monastery walls. When the monks went out in the morning they were delighted to find he was dead. Everyone was jubilantly happy. The monk in exile was hugely satisfied as well. His old values were thinning down. Nonviolence had its limits.

Ever since; his nights had been filled with dreams of far off beaches on the other side of the world. Somewhere back there he had lived another life another life time ago. There, the beaches were always long and flat and empty. Not a soul was to be seen. It was another land where the sea shone so bright blue it hurt your eyes.

Ever since he had even more trouble sleeping. An unfamiliar homesickness gripped his heart. Each morning he greeted the day with less enthusiasm than before. He knew he had another name he had almost forgotten and spoke another language on other shores. Somewhere along the line he had taken one gigantic leap of faith. In less than no time bridges had been burnt; his career was uprooted, and he was in India with his guru.

One stray LSD fuelled epiphany had been enough to uproot him. One epiphany too many. Ever since the attack he kept think about that balmy Melbourne night when a dose of clear light acid raided the unspeakable. One single heroic dose of LSD turned him inside out. It was strange to think a bunch of particular molecules could unlock paradise. Back in that forgotten life he was a scientist. He had thought of all religion as moribund irrational humbug. But one dose had back doored him into eternity where sound became colour and colour became sound. In one leaf was all revelation. Then he saw clearly that what was in the one was in the whole. Telepathy was as easy as breathing and the Garden of Eden was hiding out in plain sight. The memory of being ambushed by psychedelics kept on mocking him. Why after all the mantras and all the penance and all the yoga was a single dose of LSD still undoubtedly the single most transcendent experience of his life?

Oh the folly! He was so much younger then. So sure! Indeed the true believer, single pointed to the quest. There was only one call. Liberation. He was adamant. He who hesitates is lost.

As the monk in exile recalled that balmy night he managed a bitter sweet smile. All his hesitation had caught up with him now. He blamed Bob Dylan. And he also blamed Neil Young. It happened two weeks after the bandits attack. At first he thought it was a psychotic episode. What were the chances? How was it that he could hear Neil Young's plaintive voice in the sweltering village bazaar? Sure enough, Krishna was playing tricks on him. He could hear the Canadians plaintive voice rising above the hot blooded Bengali hustle.

"Old man take a look at my life I'm a lot like you...."

The impact stunned him. A wall of hidden memories rose up and hit him like a punch in the guts. A wave of regret and homesickness nearly doubled him over. He went straight to the music vendor and started rustling urgently through the cassettes. There was no Neil Young. Nothing but Hindi and Bengali pop songs and one solitary lost cassette of Bob Dylan's *'blood on the tracks.'* Was it a sign? He purchased the cassette, went back to the monastery and found a quiet corner away from everybody and listened closely to every single song.

Dylan was snarling his songs as he always did. He was singing out all his passion and longing and regret. He gave the monk in exile a mirror to look into. All those songs of love and loss were his. He was a man without faith now. He had been driven by idiot winds. He was tangled up in blue. He was the outcaste looking for shelter from the storm. His life had been undone by an unwanted theophany and a simple twist of fate. He was womanless and impoverished and utterly lonesome. He was yearning for everything he had burnt and lost along the way.

The monk in exile did his best to conceal his awakened unbelief from his fellow monks. They looked up to him as one of their Gurus' elite foreign disciples. But in his head the monk in exile spoke a language they would not want to hear.

He wanted to tell them that death made everything meaningless. He wanted to tell them that they could not depend on God. God played a hard game and did not follow rules. He wanted to tell them not to depend on Gurus. Gurus came with bad manners and huge egos. He wanted to tell them not to depend on philosophers. They whirled around in furious disputations unable to agree on what the head of a pin looked like. He wanted to say the quest for liberation was an illusion. They were always going to be tangled up in blue. He wanted to tell them not to trust in miracles and signs and wonders.

They were a dime a dozen until you really needed one; always here yesterday and gone tomorrow.

He no longer wanted to live inside his recklessly acquired life. The only question now was whether or not to commit suicide.

The monk in exile trudged on feeling dizzy in the delta heat. He had sorted out one question at least. By the time he got back to the monastery he was bone dry and heat struck. He burst out laughing all the same. So much for mother Ganges.

Far away there was a long, wide, empty surf beach calling him home.

8

The New Evangelist

The new convert was having trouble being a muscular believer. Witnessing for his faith and turning up to work as a junior psychiatric nurse in a maximum-security psyche ward was a high wire act. He was afraid he was doing it wrong. He didn't want to speak despite the insistence of some of the brethren back at the prayer group. He didn't want to be preachy and wag the finger. Surely just turning up was enough but some of the elders in the prayer group demurred. 'Witness in both word and deed' they commanded or else be cut off from the Lord and be lost to the darkness like that wretch who buried his talent in the ground and did nothing with it. They were quite adamant. 'Jesus was the only way and the only truth and the only life leading to salvation. There were so many souls to be saved. He must not disown the Lord under pressure or the Lord would disown him completely.' The lady who hid razor blades in her hair was having none of it.

They were watching day-time television getting numbed by sit coms. The lady who hid razor blades in her hair had a history of violence. The charge nurse said she was a monster. The new convert did not know why. She had a winsome smile and kept her hair tied up neatly in a bun. Apparently, she had slashed a female nurse not long back. It was hard to believe when she seemed so nice. Mostly they chatted about how bad the day time acting was or about cooking or the weather but when he mentioned how he liked to go to church on Sundays, it was the 'God' word that sparked her off.

"Does your God burn people forever?" She fixed him with an inquisitorial stare.

"I can't say," the new convert stammered uncomfortably. "Hell is to refuse the Lord but he is always seeking us."

"So, it is love me or burn? And you think I am bad!"

"Hell is always a choice."

"Is it? And your God supervises the torture by outsourcing it to the devil?"

"No, no, it is not like that."

"What is it like then? Three strikes and you're out! Then it is off to all that outer darkness and gnashing of teeth."

The new convert felt his conviction waning. "No, no," he protested. "God is love," he spoke quickly "but you cannot have love without the truth," he added, remembering what the elders back at the prayer group often said.

"What's that supposed to mean? For heaven's sake! Burning people forever! Wow! That takes the cake! That takes cruelty to new and unbearable levels. Is that why your religion keeps producing so many cruel people?"

The new convert was at a loss for words. The days in the unit were long. He just wanted to watch the sit coms and wear the clock down. Perhaps it was better to leave witnessing to people with more faith than himself.

He was relieved when suddenly there was a commotion and the charge nurse came running calling for help. Upstairs there was screaming and mayhem. The big Polish boy had thrown one of the staff down the stairs and was now cornered by Boris, the ward enforcer. The Polish boy was huge but Boris was bigger. All the nurses and all the patients were scared of Boris. There was a rumour he used to be a concentration camp guard back in Croatia. He had hands as big as bulldozers and a face that looked hard enough to break bricks.

By the time the other nurses arrived, Boris had the boy in a headlock and was marching him off to the locked cell room. The boy was yelling and screaming but Boris threw him against the wall like he was a rag doll. There was more yelling while the charge nurse gave the new convert the needle they needed to sedate the boy. The new convert was still rushing to prepare the needle when Boris jumped on the Polish boy's back. He heard something crack. The big boy was sobbing now while they held him down and pulled down his trousers. The new convert jabbed the boy in the bum and tried not to curse. He was all out of witness power. The Polish boy kept sobbing while they waited for the sedation to take effect. The new convert wished he was on the floor, jabbed and relieved of his senses. He was only the junior nurse who had to know his place. He had only gone nursing because some of the elders back at the prayer group reckoned he was being called to what they called ministry. It all sounded grand and heroic and uplifting. A life of witness to the saving love of the Lord. Maybe he was just not heroic enough.

Back at the charge nurse's station, the new convert slammed his finger accidentally in the drug cabinet. Uncharacteristically he let off a stream of expletives.

"Fuck! Fuck!" he wrung his hand in pain while they all fell about laughing.

"Fuck! Fuck! You actually swore!" the charge nurse laughed loudest. The new convert grimaced apologetically. His witnessing was going from bad to worse. No one had heard him use the F word before.

"I am sorry," he said sheepishly.

"No, don't be," the charge nurse laughed and patted the new convert sympathetically on the shoulder. "I know it was rough. Boris is rough. But we need Boris in a place like this. We need to say "fuck" frequently. I hope you are not so green that you don't know what fuck means. If you don't then you are fucked." The charge nurse laughed a bit too much for the new convert's liking. Then he patted the new convert's shoulder. "Why don't you take Neddy on an escort to the canteen? Let the adrenalin settle for a bit."

The new convert stammered something and then went out to look for Neddy. His blood was still fizzing. His witness was in tatters. People only laughed at him. A long slow walk with Neddy felt like just the escape he needed.

Neddy was mostly considered to be a gentle soul except for his odd rages. All the same he was on enough psychotropic medication to tranquillise an elephant. He had already been locked away for years, along with his secret messages from aliens and his drawings and his notes. Neddy rarely spoke English. Sometimes he had shown the new convert his drawings along with explanations about how he received communications from another time dimension in another galaxy. Sometimes when Neddy spoke he would tell anyone who listened about how he had been abducted and that since then he could travel backwards and forwards in time.

The new convert found Neddy hunched over and talking in his own secret language. He roused him from his corner and together they began the long stroll to the hospital canteen. Neddy as usual seemed to be off world with the aliens. The new convert walked with him and sighed. Surely here was an occasion to witness. Surely

Jesus could cut through all this madness and mayhem. Surely all it needed was a word of faith to be the bridge between Neddy and the Lord. Was he not an evangelist after all? If only he had more faith. All he had to do was reach out in the power and name of the lord. Surely then Jesus would act. Then, just as Jesus had done, he too would drive the madness and the demons away. Was not the lord inviting him to reach out now? Had not the elders commanded that he witness in season and out?

Neddy had his head down and was still mumbling when the new convert finally spoke.

He stopped Neddy, put his hand firmly on Neddy's shoulder and said with all the earnest faith he could muster:

"You know, Neddy, Jesus really loves you."

Miraculously Neddy straightened himself out of his hunch. The new convert felt excited. The Lord was at work! He looked at Neddy in amazement as he stopped mumbling and his eyes cleared. Surely it was the Lords' work. Neddy had never looked so sane. He now looked calm and composed and in his right mind. His eyes narrowed a little as they regarded the new convert for some time. The new convert waited in hushed expectation. Finally Neddy snapped, "Who the bloody hell told you that!"

The new convert was gobsmacked. The Lord was nowhere to be seen. He wished Neddy's aliens would arrive and beam him to their distant galaxy. Maybe they already knew The Lord. Neddy was still frowning irritably, clearly he was in no mood to find out.

"Fuck!" he whispered quietly to himself. Neddy was already back on the move. The new convert had to run to catch up. He knew it was time he started swearing more.

9

Gink

Every time the smell undid her. There was no disguising it. There was no perfume, no incense, no aerosol or disinfectant on God's earth that could keep it at bay. Every time she punched in the code and walked the long linoleum corridor it punched her in the head. Even before she took a step, it tore up her nose and flat lined all the way down to her guts. It was the smell of ruin, decay and death. It was the smell of her father all rheumy and withered with stroke and bed locked. How she hated it! How she could hardly bear seeing him all vacant and crumpled, his once proud jaw all slack and his mouth oozing drool. The sheer indignity! To be toothless and stuck in his own shit, breached by age, surrounded by food stains and at the mercy of strangers. No wonder she kept away. He wasn't there anymore. How could that feeble contracted wraith be her father? How on earth would anyone want to visit and suffer that smell? That cloying, sticky, insinuating stench of putrescence. Every time it undid her.

Not that she ever spoke such words even to herself. She was

busy with excuses. There was work and a family to care for. She was a grandmother now herself. There was a husband who could not dress himself properly without her. There were pets, church meetings, little athletics and a garden to care for. There were friends and responsibilities and life was hectic. And she was getting old. She didn't like admitting it but she was wearing thin, getting sketchy with fatigue and carrying too much weight. Life was a rushing river and she was flat out keeping the boat in the right direction. But all the same she knew why she kept away. It was the smell.

Not that she would ever admit it. She was not some pinched nose princess when it came to earthly odours. She didn't need a deodorized world restricted to sugar and spice and all things nice. Cat vomit and dog shit, kid's farts, horse shit spread too thick and a sweaty husband she could take in her stride.

There were other earthy smells that were divine. Like warm dry earth on a summer's day after rain and Honeysuckle on the spring breeze. And there was no smell on earth as good as the scent of her daughter's brand new baby all fresh and tender. Every time she took her in her arms she couldn't get enough of her. Unspoiled human! Still fresh with the odour of original blessing.

She only really had a need to hold her nose in the nursing home. How she hated herself for it! Her lack of grit and grace. She knew her excuses were no excuse. Eventually she would visit. If only to support her mother who had been so brave and present this whole long year. She had to admit to herself that without her mother's faithful vigil she would have stayed away more.

It had been a year since her proud father fell like a mighty oak. It was her mother who found the old warrior on the floor. His fighting days were done. The doctors were amazed he had survived. Barely. Now he was locked up inside himself with all the lights off. Now only her mother still believed there was some spark of recognition in her father's stroke numbed eyes. Now the only greeting she ever got from him were strangled moans, grunts and coughs like he was some chained and fettered beast needing to be put out of its misery. Try as she might, she could recognize next to nothing of the man who had been her hero, her protector, her sage and patron and unalloyed devotee.

She was his youngest, his little terror, his favourite amongst favourites and she knew it. No one else had gotten away with such mischief. No one else so believed all his stories; both tall and true. No one else had quite as many shoulder rides or bed time treats. It was her father not her mother who soothed her brow after getting into trouble. It was his hands that patted her apologetically and tucked her in after her mother had sanctioned her to her room. It was his smile that was the last thing she saw before the lights went out. She might have loved and respected her mother across those years but it was her father whom she adored. She was the one who broadcast all his stories at school.

She told them about his riding into aboriginal camps as a young Queensland police man and then quitting the force after witnessing the violence. He was the hero who helped rescue all those poor souls in the water after the hospital ship was torpedoed. He was the one who told her just how it felt when a torpedo went off in the water. How it shook his heart.

At school she was proud of her renaissance man; her raconteur of a father. Who else had a father with a thousand and one stories to tell? Who else was a boxer, a police man, a soldier, a builder, a jazz man and banjo player extraordinaire? Who else worked so hard and could play just as well? Who else was so smooth and rough? Who else was so brave and so dangerous? Who else was such a rebel with a cause? Who had taught her how to assess the poor and the powerful? It was her father who had flown the flag for justice and compassion even if that got a bit rough around the edges. It was her father who was so much larger than life. It was her father who was so calm in the storm and so funny before bedtime. It was her father who was her rugged prince teaching her how to wonder and marvel at the world.

As she hurried through the code she braced herself for the world on the other side of the sliding doors. She asked herself where was that man now. Did he even exist inside that locked downed ruin anymore? Where was that strong armed man? Where was that long distance swimmer whose arms held her so easily above the waves?

As she rounded the corner to her father's room she saw her mother sitting by his side like she did every day without fail. She knew her mother had other answers to her questions. Her father was still here, bound and twisted, contracted and fallen but not abandoned. Her mother did not hold her nose or stay away. Every day she came to him with her generous ration of love. She came with enough for him and some left over for the other residents that the staff told her never had any visits. Every day she would sit without fuss or tears and keep vigil. She would talk and smile and clean his mouth and face and chat about days long past. Mostly she was quiet except for her friendly chat with the carers doing their rounds. Where did she come by such love?

Her mother did not look up as she entered the room. She looked more tired than she could recall. She was drawn and slumped and her eyes looked almost as dull as her fathers. "Hello, love. Good to see you." Her mother then raised her head and made a thin attempt to smile.

"Hi, Mum." She was upbeat back, fighting back the smell and her precious repugnance. "Good to see you too." She walked over and gave her mum a peck on the cheek before sitting on the other side of the bed to take her father's hand. She gave it a squeeze and kissed his forehead. "Hi, Dad."

He said nothing. His hand limp and cold, his body inert with diminished life.

Her mother stood up. "Glad you are here, love. I'm going out for a bit. Won't be too long."

"Good oh then." She gave her mum a big bright smile doing her best to fight down her dismay. The last thing she wanted was to be left alone. To be marooned in the fetid air with no one to talk to save some shadow from the past. Now without small talk with her mother or banter with the carers, she would have to sit squarely down with all her dread and all her revulsion. She kept her game face on and kept smiling for her mother's sake. As soon as her mother was gone she squeezed her father's hand again and gave him another kiss on the cheek. "Hey, Dad, how's it going? Who are you rescuing today?" She gave his hair a brush with her hand as she spoke. Unexpectedly she reached for a tear falling down her cheek. She flicked it away annoyed with herself. When would all this sadness just go away? She bowed her head, sighed and squeezed her father's hand again. She looked away. All he was now, was just a ghost with flesh; a zombie who had checked out without notice. He was gone and he was never ever coming back.

Time dragged on. Then half asleep in the overheated air she heard someone calling her name. Surely she had heard it! Not her normal business card name. No, not that! No, it was her secret name. The name only one person in all the world had ever used. Surely she had heard it!

"Gink."

She looked up, too startled to blink. Suddenly she was a little girl again. 'Gink' was his jolly little one and only name for her. How she had sometimes stamped her feet pretending that name offended her. Especially when he sang it or said in a teasy sort of way. But every time she heard him say it in his slow drawling voice she beamed inside. She knew she was his one and only princess. She knew she was loved. It was the first name she could remember. How could she be hearing it now? It was an outrage! It was impossible! But there it was, challenging the air, exposing her soul in-between breaths.

"Gink!"

Gasping she sat bolt upright and held her father's hand in both of hers.

"Dad!" she kept gasping, wondering if she had heard right. She surveyed his face. Was that a squeeze she could feel in his heavy old hand? Was she seeing things? Was there a fluttering fleeting light coming at her from the depths of his eyes. An urgent light burning with a brief audacious lucid intensity.

It was! She heard it again!

"Gink!"

And then he spoke, more a gasp and a croak or a moan but she heard alright.

"You know, Gink, there is only love."

She heard him whisper it. Tender and true in the grey afternoon.

And that was that. The light submerged again. The day wore on but she had seen and heard it. A strange miracle had detached itself from the other end of the known world and had come visiting.

Her father's jaw went slack again. The smell hung as it always did. It no longer mattered.

There was only love.

10

The Antipodean Pilgrim

The antipodean came apart somewhere between the alpha and the omega. There should have been clear warning signs; 'mind the gap, enter at own risk.' He blamed the lax security at Chartres cathedral. They let any mug pilgrim walk the labyrinth path there unsupervised. It was presumed you brought your own God. The armchair brochures back home promised safe passage. People got lost in mazes not labyrinths. The centre would hold, the six-pointed rose would receive and renew all creation. Everyone would be saved, one step at a time.

It was too good to be true and he should have known it. No one warned him about the edge giving way or about being dissolved. No one told him he might disappear entirely. No one mentioned anything about dying. No one mentioned how far out you had to walk to find your way in. It was presumed you brought your own faith.

Four days later and having a nervous breakdown at Charles de Gaul airport he knew did not have enough. Europe had done him in. His ancestors had all gone missing. He was nothing but a mote of dust floating in a sea of strangers. The labyrinth had given voice to stone and air. He belonged neither to the new world or the old. He was homeless and alone and at the mercy of a God who wrote straight with crooked lines. He was a huddled quaking mess afraid of history. Everywhere in Europe the stones cried out. They all had blood drenched stories. The fair city of Paris was not what she seemed. Beneath the chic exterior was a pain-soaked history. Everywhere he went everything was contrived, shaped and modified by a heavy human hand. Nothing was untamed. What was in one was in the whole. The very air felt claustrophobic. There were too many generations on top of each other. Beneath her sexy appeal the beautiful city was stained and bloated with the cruelties and pretensions of empire.

To be fair, the labyrinth was not entirely to blame. From day one it had been allergy at first sight. The Louvre kick-started it all. It was there the empire was seen in all its bloated, overdressed finery. As he wandered through gallery after gallery, he felt a hunger for simple beauty growing. He felt like a runaway slave gazing at the dead bodies of old slave masters. There was nothing fresh or open or uncluttered to be seen. The stale beauty made him feel like he was asphyxiating in a cloud of perfume. He became desperate for fresh air and warm sun.

The grand churches of Notre Dame and Sacre Coeur did not improve his mood. They felt like shrines to Caesar rather than sanctuaries for the carpenter. They were tight with tourists and light on for pilgrims.

The antipodean had not long come from Uluru. There, sharp blue skies and the shape shifting many coloured monolith was a match for all the cathedrals of Europe. The spinifex grass and iron-red earth kept him good company. The nights were a dream scape of innumerable stars. Nothing prepared him for so much immensity. For a whole day he walked around it in stunned awe. It was like arriving at the centre of the world. It was like touching the central chakra point holding all things together. The monolith felt larger than all human history. Its grandeur went deep; all the way down the bones of the earth, where the centre was everywhere and the circumference nowhere to be seen.

For a brief moment he was complete and whole. For a brief moment he felt held and embraced in primal blessing. He was no longer a stranger in a strange land. Even if his ancestors were from far away, here there was space to spare. For a brief moment he began to know who he really was. But then he went and spoiled it all by catching a plane to Europe. He should have known better.

Chartres cathedral was the real deal compared to the painted churches of Paris. Like Uluru it stood on ancient sacred ground. Like Uluru the stone felt alive. The circular rose windows also held the world in a great belonging. It felt like a sanctuary not a tourist trap. Once inside he lost perspective. The great arched ceiling floated out of sight. He could feel the prayers of generations vaulting to impossible heights in the shadowed air. The muted light coming through the rose windows transcended sermons. The labyrinth awaiting him in the nave was empty but full of promise. Uluru and its many colours no longer felt like it was on the far side of the world. It felt perfectly safe to enter.

At first the going was easy. Soon he caught sight of the sacred centre. It was impossible to get lost. He knew all he had to do was put one foot after another. All he had to do was stop thinking and be silent. That was when all the trouble started. It started with making comparisons. He looked up when he should have looked down. Before he knew it he was talking to himself. Before he knew it, he was nothing but one loud and rude rush of thought.

The antipodean blamed another pilgrim for his distraction. She was a picture of sheer graceful mindfulness, taking the path to reality's centre one deliberate step at a time. She held her head still as she walked with her eyes half closed. She looked so beautiful, so elegant, so poised, so centred and so unhurried. She appeared outside of time. Her movement felt seamless; like some Theravada forest monk feeling out the world through her feet. She was one with the flow and at home in her own skin. Her tread was slow and sure, content with each moment at a time. The antipodean couldn't take his eyes off her.

The antipodean tried to look down not up. At some point the labyrinth spiral stretched out of shape. It felt like he was free falling into sheer nothingness. He was taking steps alright but he was on the way to death and nowhere.

The comparisons kept coming with each step, amplified by the mocking accusers his mind brought along for the ride. They were all joyless, cruel and vicious. They told him he was all talk and no walk. He was inelegant, unpoised, ugly, unbalanced, ignorant, anxious, vain and ungrounded. He was taking steps but going backwards. He was all head and no heart. He was a fraud and an empty gong booming and only death awaited. She was at one with it all. He was cut off from it all. He should have kept his head down.

The antipodean was half way through the labyrinth before he looked down rather than up. By then it was too late. The murmuring mockers were a full-throated chorus. He was a nobody from the ends of the earth. He belonged nowhere. His ancestors were all ghosts who had disowned him. God played dice and the universe was essentially unsafe and unfriendly. And somewhere, just out of sight, just out of range, was a thorny whisperer saying; "skin for skin."

By the time he got to the rose petal centre he felt like he had run a marathon. He felt like he had lived too long already. He was lost, not found, and instead of a labyrinth he had wandered into a maze where the world on cue was ending without a bang or even a whimper.

By the time he caught the train to Paris the world had gone dark. He was not prepared for such loss of faith. It was a warm August day but he felt chilled to the bone. Christ had gone missing on him inside the labyrinth. Perhaps Christ had never heard of the antipodes. Perhaps Christ had long since left Europe. Perhaps everything happened for no reason at all and life was essentially meaningless. The labyrinth had taken him to the centre but the centre had not held. He had to keep walking in any case. He was just another tourist with trains to catch and with time and money to waste.

The antipodean spent the next three days catatonically prone in his hotel. His allergic reaction to Europe now full blown. Never had he felt so lonely and inconsequential. Still the voices kept on whispering. Was it God or was it the devil? He had no way of knowing. Was it a whispered command or just a whispered curse?

"Skin for skin."

At Chartres no one warned him just how difficult God and the devil could be. At Charles de Gaul airport no one cared. Life was a relentless thing until it wasn't. Schedules must be kept, destinations arrived at and business made usual. It was as good a place as any to have a full-scale nervous breakdown.

The antipodean sat and watched all the strangers mill past. A cleaner eyed him suspiciously, like he might be some piece of refuse missed in the clean-up. Everywhere there were people who belonged to someone else. They were solid, tactile and filled with purpose. They lived in some other world under an unfettered sun. They were pilgrims, lovers, workers, players, hustlers and grifters. They all had stories and ancestors. He almost wept with envy.

Only the suspicious cleaner had eyes for him. He felt invisible, like a wraith dissolving into the shadows. A flight crew came past with flat faces ready to switch to game mode. A group of Muslim pilgrims came past rustling prayer beads. A young couple embraced like long lost kin. Even if God had disappeared the world kept turning. Only he was alone.

The antipodean was disappearing into the dark when a young girl came skipping by with her mother. She was as sure footed and at home with herself as any forest monk. She was bouncy and chatty and bright with colour. They were almost out of sight when he heard the little girl speak one of the few French words he knew. It dropped out of the air like a summons:

"*Merci.*"

The antipodean stood up. He had a plane to catch. A word had been given. The gift of a random kindness. He didn't know what it meant but it was the only solid thing he had to go on. One single word survived the labyrinth.

"*Merci.*"

The antipodean pilgrim stopped talking to himself and started walking. There was no other way out of Europe.

11

The Bad Mother

Her yoga teacher was quite adamant. There was no such thing as an accident. He would brook no dissent. Every person authored their own reality. Everyone had some karma they were working out. Everyone was called to be enlightened. Everyone needed to become mindful and one-pointed enough to be master of their own destiny. Only the ignorant had accidents. Every accident was nothing more than the result of spiritual failure. So, there was nothing else for it then. She had to be a bad mother.

The police did not quite agree. Her son's death was an accident they said although they hinted speed might have been a factor along with brake failure. They were very sensitive about it all. It was just one of those things they said. Anything was liable to go wrong on a dark winding road on a black winter's night. Young men were liable to believe they were invincible. All the same, accidents happened.

Her yoga teacher came to her highly recommended. Some of her female friends spoke in hushed tones about how he had been an Olympic standard gymnast and was a Vietnam veteran. They murmured about how muscular and handsome he was and how he did not suffer fools. Laggards, pretenders and dabblers were frequently ejected from his classes. Not for him some gentle stretching. He was an alpha yogi who pushed his students to breaking point. If you did not pay complete attention you were shown the door and not invited back.

Like some of her hushed friends she made sure she paid attention. She was not going to be one of those hapless disciples he humiliated. She liked the way her teacher was so focused, rigorous and intense. She liked the way he prowled around his class with the sinewy litheness of a caged panther. When he held them for a long time in a pose, she would dig deep for the strength to surrender to it. Every time she felt her limits were being stretched further, her teacher would say she had more to give. Failure was for cowards he said. It is always simple he said. Just become awakened, and you will master your destiny.

She had not gone back since her darling boy had crashed into a tree. Clearly, she was a failure. Clearly her karma was all her fault. It was too much to bear. There had to be some other reason, some other explanation. Some other guru more forgiving, some kinder dispensation. Where was her beautiful darling boy now? Why were the heavens so silent? Why could she not see his face anymore? How could he disappear so completely?

Her flirtation with yoga was recent. For years she and her husband spurned all forms of organized religion. They were all for living in the now. She was a long way past the good Anglican grammar school believer of her youth. Every census she adopted a different religion or just made one up. Atheist wasn't that original. Jedi was passé. White witch felt a bit too over the top. Sufi Zen Baptist had a good ring to it though. She and her husband had a laugh about it. Life was too short to get twisted out of shape by hand-me-down ideologies. The yoga had come along as a surprise. There were some questions brewing after all. Anyway, she was spiritual not religious.

Not now.

Now all her twisty questions haunted her. Now she needed some sort of thing that could bring all the broken pieces together. There was no rest. Her yoga teacher was wrong and so were the police. They could not show her where her boy was. Could anyone?

The priest at the funeral didn't seem to know much. He was a kind man; more than willing to meet them half way, which wasn't like a lot of priests she heard of. He didn't mind unchurched Anglicans coming to a Catholic priest for the rites. 'We are all family,' he said. 'We are all blind pilgrims helping each other.'

It wasn't alpha guru stuff. The priest told them all that 'life was changed, not ended'. She felt he was saying something someone else had thought out for him. She could feel a yawning gap between his rhetoric and reality. What could a man without original insight know about loss and grief? What did he know about parenting or the contrariness of God? His second-hand faith was hardly faith at all.

Her husband barely bothered listening. For him the priest was just another cog turning the wheels of the death industry. He hid behind his pooncey robes while the poker-faced undertakers remained armour plated behind their pin-striped suits. They smiled kindly at all the right times but their compassion was for hire. Grief is costly after all. She and her husband waved the funeral attendants and the priest goodbye. They were content to leave the tab with them and move on. She and her husband would be paying it off for the rest of their lives.

On the way out to the hearse it was all she could do to stop her husband punching out one of the attendants scrolling through his phone with an insouciant disregard for the occasion. Her husband had a history of violence. He had been the original wild thing until she tamed him. They came from opposite ends of town. She was the good grammar school girl from the genteel classes. He was underclass. What was she to do? He was so drop-dead good looking back in his day; just like her darling boy. They were like Romeo and Juliet. They turned their back on the preachy hostility from her family. She gave them the finger along with the Anglican establishment and took her life on a wild turn. Together they banged and balled their way across the country. They partied hard and lived dangerously. Was that why she was punished now? After all she was just another good girl unable to resist a bad man. It took quite a long ride to work her alchemy and change her wild, street fighting man into a caring mate and loving father.

Little by little her wild man changed from a brawling builder's labourer to sensitive new age aesthete. Well almost. Her magic had its limits. Rather it was the birth of their darling boy which changed base metal into gold. The day her son was born her husband was abjectly and deliriously happy. From then on they did not look back. Two girls followed and they became a family, navigating the world together. Only her mother struck a kind of sour note:

"Well dear, now you will discover one of life's hard truths, we all have to get tamed and nothing will tame you like having a child."

She hated hearing that and refused to believe it. Her boy had not tamed her; he had called her to be who she really was. Carer, giver, creator, enabler and mother. Instead of resenting motherhood she embraced it with all her soul. But now, soul and heart were in pieces. The whole world was riven ever since brake failure on a dark, dark winter's night.

The day of the funeral was a blur of desolation. None of the hired kindness gave comfort. Her only consolation was when a proud magpie strutted into the sanctuary and stopped them all in their tracks while it warbled in rapt melody. She hung on to it as a sign. When she told her husband, he just snorted.

"Bloody hell woman! Stop believing bullshit and seeing things that aren't there."

But she had too much pain-soaked longing to stop. After the funeral a yawning divide grew between them. Grief made them ghosts to each other. Against her husband's advice she decided to become religious rather than spiritual and went on a church crawl. He went on a pub crawl instead.

She became a faith tourist looking for signs and wonders.

Her husband become morose and angry looking for ways to forget. Whenever she told him about a sign or a wonder that just might make sense, his response was always the same. He would curse and snort;

"Bloody bullshit woman!"

It did not stop her looking. She kept doing the rounds. She went back to the Anglicans. They were cake and tea polite and nice enough. They offered chatty comfort and kept their distance. She went to the Pentecostal mega church and got love bombed on the way in. She tried to raise her arms in praise with the rest of them but gave up when they said bad things happen when you do not have enough faith. She went to the Catholics who ignored her entirely except for the sign of peace. No one even asked her name and she went home lonelier than when she arrived. She went to mediums and psychics. They always seemed sincere and convincing but their secrets always came with a price tag. Every time she came back from one of them her husband would say it again.

"Bloody bullshit woman!"

Her sister even took her to a little catholic rosary group. The old ladies were very sweet and kind. They told her how 'Our lady' had been sending the world warnings to repent. They taught her the Fatima Prayer which they prayed devoutly. But she didn't like the way they were always praying to be saved from the fires of hell. When she told them she didn't want her darling boy to be burn in those fires they patted her gently and said because she was a woman of faith her son would be saved. She should not worry. Her boy was a bright angel now, one who along with 'Our lady' would always intercede for her in this valley of tears. It was a comfort too cold to bear. She left the sweet old ladies to their God and went looking for another church. When she told her husband what they had said he was even more furious.

"Bloody fucking bullshit woman!"

A few nights later she went to bed weeping while the magpies said their evening prayers. At some time in the lonely watches of the night she was run over by a dream.

It was her darling boy! Changed somehow. Somehow he seemed more alive. More himself than she had ever seen him. He was so gorgeous. A shining avatar, with eyes so deep brown she could drop off the known edges of the world and be lost in them forever. He was close and he was worlds away. God how could he be so beautiful?

She wanted him to speak, to say something but he was in the place beyond all words. Instead, he gave her a stunning radiant smile and pointed to the bible beside her bed. She woke up gasping and shook her husband awake.

"Oh woman!" he groaned too tired to be angry. But she was determined he should know about her lucid dream. He kept softly cursing but she shook him again and made him pick up the bible beside their bed.

"Open it!" she insisted.

"Where?" he was getting cross.

"I don't know, just as it falls. Read to me what you see." She knew she couldn't bear to look herself.

Her husband kept groaning. He opened the book anyway and

marked a passage he saw already indented and separate from the rest of the text:

Naked I came from my mother's womb
Naked I shall return
The Lord gives,
The Lord takes,
Blest be the name of the Lord.

The dawn was not far off. Somewhere close a magpie sang in the day. They fell into each other arms weeping.

The magpies kept on singing and singing.

12

The Forward Scout

"Get down! Get down! The Japs are coming!"

The old veteran never used to speak about the war. His daughters never asked him and his wife knew not to. Now she was gone he had no reason to keep his mind. Grief and gravity brought back all the ghosts. One fall too many collapsed the gap between past and present. Ever since they found him on the floor with broken hip and shoulder, he had lost all interest in the present. Life was one outrage after another. His wife's death, his consignment to a nursing home, his fall, followed by surgery and infection and being held captive by pain. It was time to surrender to yesterday and his waking dreams.

He was back in Bougainville. He was a forward scout sniper. He was twenty and already a veteran of forgotten battles. He was way out past the perimeter line slung up in his hammock shrouded in vines and mosquitoes waiting and waiting. There was no nursing home anymore only the pitiless dark of the jungle, the boredom and the gnawing suspense. He was death in waiting. His mates knew he was touched. Some called him mad. They reckoned he was moved and protected by strange angels. What sort of mad bastard would actually volunteer to be a scout! Some thought it was good luck to be around him. They reckoned he might have gone cold killer crazy the way he blended into the night and came back with more kill notches on his belt. Sometimes he was gone for days touched by rage and terror. Each time he returned he felt that little less human and each time he got back he couldn't wait to go back out again. Sometimes he had to be extra careful not to be shot by his own sentries. It was part of the deal of being on the wrong side of the perimeter line.

It was not a fair fight. The Japs in against eight thousand Australians in a back water battle no one else wanted to remember. It was a slow hard kill. The bastards refused to surrender and here they were, in a useless mongrel dog-fight, while the front-line glory boys rolled the Japs all the way back to the land of the rising sun.

It was a fight they never really won. It took a mushroom cloud to do it. They got the news late. Some blokes had seen newsreels of victory parades and shots of the Yanks making the Japs surrender on one of their bloody battleships giving the Nips in coattails a lesson in humility.

But on Bougainville the war haemorrhaged on. The Japs kept fighting as they always did. His waking dreams still shifted and bled.

He was by the river. A conscript not a volunteer. For days they had been blaring messages over loudspeakers and air dropping leaflets telling the imperial army the unthinkable had happened. The empire was no more. Stop fighting.

His luck must have been running out. His captain had volunteered him to be in the company sitting out in the open like sitting ducks while they broiled and fretted in the hot sun. For three days they sat out bored shitless and itchy with fear. No one was in a mood for mercy. The white flag seemed too good for the sneaky, shifty, cruel yellow bastards. The only way you negotiated with them was by killing them. How could anyone forget all that atrocity, pain and mayhem? How do you stop the rage and the terror? What remains after you have walked through fire and blood?

His waking dreams were a dream within a dream. None of them believed it was over. Even when the Japanese officer finally made his appearance they did not believe it. With his head held erect and his samurai sword it seemed he had too much courage and dignity to look like a man beaten. Even with his uniform trashed and reduced to skin and bone he looked in charge. Beaten and defeated but unbowed. How he hated him until he drew close and looked into the officer's eyes. They were soldier's eyes just like his; bruised and burnt and weary with war. Seeing that man with his eyes filled with loss drained him of rage. Then when the stragglers came out of the jungle rat thin in rags, wounds festering and with all the light gone from their eyes, he had no more hatred left. The poor bastards! They were all mute with shock and disbelief. Just like him; they appeared to be asking questions from the silent sky. How could a world so broken ever be made new again?

It was his bad luck to go from warrior to prison guard playing nurse maid while they organized repatriation. He resented it completely. Not hating anymore did not mean forgiveness. How he resented not being home in time for all the victory parties. No one could care less about the boys from Bougainville.

But then a light entered his waking dreams. He was back home; his last day in uniform on a bright breezy day in sunny trashy Sydney. A nurse in uniform was waltzing down the street with a group of friends just in time for her to catch his eye. She was shining and he was dazzled enough to risk his luck. He could feel the mood all around. The victory parties were over. Euphoria had lost its traction. People were tired of just surviving. They had had their fill of austerity, rations, blackouts and grief. A new world now beckoned. Debts had to be paid and the wheel of industry kept turning. There were new allies and new threats on the horizon. His war was one war too many to remember. He felt the mood and so he seized his chance.

"Wanna dance," he flashed his best raffish smile and dipped his slouch hat like a gentleman. She didn't even break stride.

"Nah," she grinned. "I only go out with sailors." She laughed and teased him enough with her backwards glance.

"Okay then, where do I enlist?" He wasn't going to die wondering. He was tall and lean and cheeky and he could see she had a thing for men in uniforms. He drew alongside and fell in love with her shy smile and red hair. "Where do you work?" He was persistent.

"Saint Vinnies."

Two days later there was a dance. The rest was history. They got married, had kids and built a life until in death she departed. She never asked him about the war he always wanted to forget. She saw the night sweats, the bad dreams, the rolling battles with malaria. She knew that some things can't be said. Life rolled on and memory got blunted until the fall.

The light faded again as it had done before. Once again he was old and skinny and bed ridden. There were faces looking over him. Was it his daughter or a nurse? He couldn't even remember his own name.

Until just one solitary mosquito on a sultry afternoon brought it all back. It blitzed his ear opening up the past. It was an ambush! He sat up suddenly in a shock of movement that stunned the faces looking over him.

"Get down, get down," he gripped one of them so tightly she cried out with pain. "The Japs! The Japs are coming," and together they slid off the bed!

His daughter could not understand what was going on. She never thought about asking and now it was all too late. It was all she could do to help cushion his fall.

"It's okay now, Dad. No one is here but us," she did her best to comfort.

One of the nurses came quickly to her aid. She held her father's head and patted him gently.

"It's okay now Jimmy, it is okay. The war is over now," she soothed and smiled.

He looked up and grinned his old raffish smile. The light was back again bright and shining. He could see his wife in uniform and he was going to a dance.

13

The Chess Players

The serial killer and the hitman were playing chess when they heard the new chaplain arrive. They loathed and despised each other. They were methodical men, expert at concealing weapons and feelings. They were good at the long game. Doing consecutive life sentences lends itself to that kind of thing. They had a knack for being charming and polite. They believed that revenge was always a dish best served cold and in keeping your friends close and enemies even closer.

They did not have any friends.

It was the new chaplain's first visit to the maximum-security unit. The serial killer and the hitman were out of their cells in the cramped yard they shared for exercise. Sound travelled easily. The serial killer smiled to himself. Here was fresh sport, fresh grounds for contempt. He despised everyone but there were some he happily despised more than others; like the hitman for instance. The bloated, boastful cunning old man revolted him to his core. The serial killer figured that like everyone else, the hitman did not deserve to live.

The blotched violent retard should have been on the street when his assault rifle was in his hands. There was one that got away from him. It was a matter of deep regret the police stopped him when they did. He was convinced the world was filled with people living meaningless lives. They were pathetic, needy, selfish and despicable. Humanity was a plague that needing culling. The hitman clearly was a case in point. The serial killer knew there was a bounty on the old man's head. He would be pleased to do the deed for pleasure. The serial killer was a patient man. He smiled as he heard the prison officer greet the new chaplain and made the first move.

"How are you?" the chaplain sounded nervous and scared. Both men smiled knowingly. The new padre would have to learn about asking stupid questions.

One of the officers made his feelings known.

"I am as about as fucking happy as a Roman Catholic priest in a fucking orphanage." The serial killer giggled. The hitman kept a straight face. They heard doors being unlocked and keys jangling.

Another inmate yelled out loudly, "Hey padre! You look shit scared. What's wrong with you? Got no balls? Better grow some soon or fucking skulk somewhere else!"

The chaplain mumbled an apology they couldn't hear. The hitman made his move and met the serial killer's eyes. They both smiled. It was sport for sure. The serial killer made a counter move.

"Where is the other padre?" the same inmate kept on yelling. "He had balls! Fuck off! If you are as shit scared as you look!"

The chess players exchanged smiles that never reached their eyes. They did not like the old chaplain. He was a truck of a man with bulldozer sized hands. He had a face that looked tough enough to break bricks. Nearly all the prisoners liked the old chaplain who never seemed like he was afraid of anyone. He never gave the hitman and the serial killer the time of day. A green, bleeding-heart do-gooder was just what the day needed. The hitman made another move and kept his eyes unreadable. It was game on.

The hitman used to enjoy his work. He considered it both business and pleasure. He had a long history of violence. He knew he could take the serial killer any time he wanted. He could pull the vexatious little weed. Back in the day he would have done it for free. He too was a patient man with a reputation for success. He was good at making people disappear. The detestable weed would have to keep guessing. He would not know the day or the hour. All the same the hitman slept with one eye open. They had different cells but it was the first time he was in a unit with someone as murderous as himself. He waited for the serial killer to make another move. They heard another door unlock. The sport had arrived.

The new chaplain was small. He had small hands and frightened eyes. The guards left him to it. Both men kept their heads down, noticing everything. The chaplain looked lost but didn't look like he was stopping. They both looked up and caught his eye.

"Hi, how are you?" the new chaplain was still asking stupid questions.

The hitman and the serial killer moved their smiles closer to their eyes.

"Hello Father." The hitman was exceptionally polite. He used to be an altar boy.

The chaplain stopped, relieved that someone wanted to talk to him. "How is the game going?"

The serial killer and the hitman stood up and came to the grill of their exercise yard. "Good," the serial killer was all smiles. "Combat has only just begun." He made an extravagant gesture to the chess board. "Do you know why we play chess?" He grinned at the new chaplain's blank look.

"I don't play chess." The chaplain attempted a grin of his own.

"Only one reason." The serial killer flashed his warmest smile. "To destroy your opponent's mind."

"Oh!" The new chaplain shifted his weight uneasily.

The hitman broke in changing the topic. "Don't take the officers too seriously. It's a stressful job." He managed to strike the right note of concern. He gave the chaplain an unctuous smile. It's best to not to react and turn the other cheek. It will take you a while to learn how to get with the flow. You do look very anxious." The hitman looked as concerned as he sounded.

"I am." The chaplain figured it was better to admit it. "It is my first solo visit to the slot."

"Ah," both the hitman and the serial killer sounded sympathetic. "Welcome to the top end of town where all the big fish are." The hitman managed to sound cheerful and friendly.

"So why don't you play chess?" the serial killer segued back to his question.

"Just not sharp or smart enough," the chaplain admitted.

"Ah, what a pity" the serial killer sounded disappointed.

"So, who is winning or who is destroying who?" the chaplain tried to make his voice sound light.

The chess players exchanged unreadable looks.

"We don't know yet," the hitman smiled broadly. "We have a long way to go. Some kills are best done slow."

"Oh." The new chaplain tried not to look menaced. He made to move on. The serial killer and the hitman were not on his list to visit.

"So what do you reckon about this?" the serial killer stepped closer to the grill and pulled a card out of his sleeve, eyes shining with excitement.

The chaplain stood back warily. Both men noticed. He took the card and was unable to stop a gasp of surprise. He looked twice to be sure. Out of thin air, the serial killer had conjured a traditional catholic devotional holy card. There he was, all air brushed and saccharine holy. It was none other than Monsignor Josemaria Escriva, the founder of the conservative catholic order Opus Dei.

The chaplain gave the card back quickly. He could not manage to conceal his revulsion for Opus Dei and its pro fascist origins.

The serial killer stepped right up to the grill. He smiled as if butter would not melt in his mouth. He looked the new chaplain up and down and conjured the card out of sight. His eyes shone with malice.

"I thought we had killed off all your kind long ago."

The chaplain decided to keep his head down and move. He felt something dark and cold grip his guts. The serial killer did not veil the murder in his eyes. Murderous spirits were abroad under the prim patronage of a haloed crusader.

"Oh well," the hitman managed to sound both polite and concerned at the same time. He gave the new chaplain a knowing wink. "It looks like you are going to need protection now."

The chess players were all smiles.

Except for their eyes.

14

The Grey Nomad

The grey nomad was sick of talking to himself. He had been on the road so long and was going nowhere. There was so much of it! Threatening on every side. Mile after mile of flattened down emptiness. Minute by minute the brown water-starved land flashed by in a fearful, forlorn blur. He couldn't imagine anyone wanting to live there. The great Australian road trip no longer seemed such a good idea. Somewhere between the idea and the reality he was longing for walled gardens and bland suburbia again. He increased his speed and kept talking. It was one way not to become hypnotized by the road.

The day was wearing on. Outside his protective wind screen the world looked skun back and inhospitable. Even with air con on it felt oppressive. The grey nomad imagined it getting so hot that even the flies would go underground. He pressed on, dreaming of tropical blue-green seas, cool oases and manicured lawns. Any place not so null and empty. Any place but here.

A few kilometres later he found evidence to the contrary. A

whole chain gang of men were working by the road in the hot sun. They were all aboriginal with just a solitary white man in charge. At first He was so shocked he almost ran off the road. A moment later the chain gang disappeared in his rear vision mirror. The shock of it made him start shouting. He wondered if he was having a fevered hallucination. Whose country was he in? Had he crossed some barrier of time and space into the deep red neck south of the USA? Was it possible such a thing could be in contemporary Australia?

The chain gang had answers he did not want to hear. It was Australia and such outrages had been going on ever since the first peoples had become the last and the last were now all too evidently the first. The grey nomad grimaced thinking that Jesus had once said something about all that but somehow it had become lost in translation.

The road stretched on remorselessly .The grey nomad couldn't stop shouting. History was written by conquerors. Here he was; day tripping past slave gangs, just another pasty conqueror fast talking the land to null and empty. He drove a bit faster hoping to outrun himself. His ancestors were ruthless people. They didn't have any qualms about reverse engineering divine writ. So what if Jesus displayed a soft spot for the underside of history. Everyone knew the meek did not inherit the earth. It was never okay with the conquerors. The letter of the law was more important than its spirit. They were making sure the first were now last and the last were always first. His people had chain-ganged slaves toiling in the sun to prove it.

The grey nomad couldn't shake the sight. Back in the bland suburbs they kept evil behind picket fences and drawn curtains. The meek were discouraged from becoming an eyesore. It was far too inconvenient. He pressed on, upping his speed, mauling down the miles. No matter how much he talked he could not make the sight go away.

A little later when the grey nomad saw an aboriginal hitchhiker in dusty jeans and a tattered white T-shirt he knew he had to stop.

"Hey bro," the hitchhiker flashed the grey nomad a big ethanol infused smile. "Where ya goin?"

"North."

The grey nomad found himself light on for words. The hitchhiker swayed and smiled in the hot sun and opened the door to get in. The grey nomad did not want to say it was guilt rather than kindness which made him stop. The hitchhiker didn't appear to notice. He gave a little contented grunt and gestured at the open road "Good! Going towards my country."

The grey nomad started driving. He was in no mood for a conversation.

"So bro, what ya up to?"

"Nothing much, just a road trip."

"Good eh? Good to be out in country."

The grey nomad did not agree so he said nothing. He just nodded politely. He had no idea where he was going and thought the hitchhiker was unreasonably cheerful.

The hitchhiker was undeterred. "So where about north?"

The grey nomad thought it was a good question. What was he doing? Why was he here? Maybe he was hoping for a hint of Eden. Evidently, he was in the wrong place. Maybe he was just as advertised; just another cashed-up white fella wasting time and money, ignoring slave gangs by the road. "Maybe the ocean. Got a bit of driving still to do."

"Ah! Sounds good." The hitchhiker sighed and looked sort of wistful. Then he suddenly waved his arms about at the passing scrub. He smiled and laughed and gave the grey nomad a poke.

"It's all here, bro! My country, yeah." The hitchhiker gave a big wave of his hand. "Plenty of space out here. Plenty."

The grey nomad thought so much space was overrated. He was

not convinced. He gave his hitchhiker a dismissive grunt and kept driving.

The hitchhiker kept on smiling widely. "Nah bro, lots of good space. Plenty. More than ya need!"

The grey nomad gave the hitchhiker a long look. It was clear the hitchhiker saw something he did not.

The hitchhiker looked him full in the eye. "Yeah bro, my country. Lots of good space here. Good tucker. Good."

"It looks a bit too worn and battered for me."

"Nah, only to white fellas. This my country. Yeah. My country. Yeah."

The grey nomad said nothing. He wondered how much his passenger had to drink. His smile was too generous to be just about grog. He was a man who knew where he belonged. It made him really wonder who was last and who was first.

They drove on. Every now again the hitchhiker would give the grey nomad another pat and wave and say, "My country, yeah. My country."

The grey nomad was in no doubt who was last and who was first. He caught sight of the gleam in the hitchhiker's eye. He was not a man flying bubble wrapped over deserts. He was at home in his own skin. The grey nomad was surprised to be feeling something like jealousy. He was just the left over remains of mongrel conquerors. Unlike the hitchhiker, the grey nomad did not know where he belonged.

A bit further on the hitchhiker got the grey nomad to stop. It seemed they had stopped in the middle of nowhere. The hitchhiker was still smiling. He swayed out of the car and then reached across to shake the grey nomad's hand.

"Good bro, this my country, lots of space yeah! See ya again eh?" He gave the nomad another wave and walked off. Nowhere was all the grey nomad could see where ever he looked.

He drove on more slowly.

Further on boab trees began appearing. They were audacious in their big bellied elegance with their thin limbs acclaiming the sky. One particularly massive boab made him stop the car and step out. It was magnificently huge and all at home in its own skin. The grey nomad could see other pilgrims had passed this way. The boab was tattooed with graffiti to prove it. Its silence made the grey nomad start talking again. Instead of talking to himself he questioned the boab tree.

'How much do I really need? Where do I want to go? Why does this emptiness frighten me? Where do I belong'?

The boab tree seemed proud of its own scars. The desert wind blew, the boab's branches reached for the silence.

'Nowhere but here' was all it said.

The grey nomad stopped talking and drove on.

That night by the ocean there was a lunar eclipse. The iron red moon fell to earth undressing herself in the desert air. She was drunk with ochre light and she too had only one thing to say.

'Nowhere but here.'

15

The Boxer

The boxer never knew what day it was. His head hurt all the time and he found it hard to talk. Thinking wasn't easier. Where was he? Who was shaking him awake? Who had stolen all his clothes?

"Hey Bob, time to get up and shower, your clothes are in the locker by your bed."

The boxer rubbed sleep from his eyes and tried to sit up. Hard fluorescent light made him wince. He had difficulty focusing. With an effort he swung out of bed. He looked around for the bloke who had rudely woken him. Where was the bastard? Who were all those old men shuffling around? Some of them were wearing pyjamas just like himself. Some of them were naked. The boxer could hear water running. One of the shuffling men had fallen over. He had a gummy leg and kept cursing loudly.

"Up the camel's arse! Up the camel's arse!"

No one paid the least bit of attention. The man with the gummy leg just went on thrashing around and cursing. The boxer did not like the look of it at all. Why were his clothes missing? Why was he shaking so much? Did the Salvos have him again?

The hard linoleum floor stirred memory. Yesterday was entirely a blur but there were fragments of other lives that still visited. There had been other dormitories, other hard floors, hard lights, hard cramped places and hard nights spent sleeping rough. Punch drunk memories disappearing to mist as soon as he went looking for them.

He bunched his fists and felt some kind of knowledge returning. There was strength in his fingers. He was not old like these other blokes. He knew he could fight. He stood up shaking. Where was that bloke who woke him? The bloke who woke him looked dodgy in his grey pants and white shirt. Was he a salvo? He didn't look like one. Had he been dumped in some hostel? Who had stolen his clothes?

The boxer had to sit straight down again. Why couldn't he feel his feet properly? Where had that white shirt bastard gone? Nothing felt right, nothing at all.

"Hey Bob, time to grab a shower, your clothes are in your locker when you come back out. Leave your pyjamas here. I'll make your bed." The white shirt was back, all smiles, like butter wouldn't melt in his mouth.

"Up the camel's arse, up the camel's arse!" the man with the gummy leg kept cursing.

The boxer knew something wasn't right. He'd been dumped and the white shirt bastard must have stolen his clothes. The boxer watched him squat down and try to get hold of the man on the ground.

"Hey Ken," the white shirt was laughing now. "No camels here, just your arse. So get it off the floor."

"Up the camel's arse!" The man with the gummy leg kept cursing.

The boxer did not like the look of it one bit. That dodgy white shirt bloke wasn't a Salvo. They must have dumped him. He kept his fists bunched. His head was swimming. He must have been drinking again but couldn't remember having a drink. Bits of memory came and went through the throbbing mist in his head. He was a boxer. He did not take a flogging from any man. He knew how to work hard, drink hard, fight hard. Why did he feel so crook? Who had dumped him here and stolen his clothes? The boxer bunched and unbunched his fingers feeling his anger rise.

"C'mon, Ken." The white shirt let go of the man with a gummy leg and let him slide back down to the floor. They both ended on the linoleum. The boxer watched on angrily. The white shirt was still laughing. He was playing games! He was dodgy! He was a thief! He needed a flogging!

The boxer tried to stand up again but his legs didn't work properly.

"C'mon, Ken, team effort." The white shirt was trying to get the man with a gummy leg to move again. "Maybe we need one or two camels after all. Here we go, slow and steady. One, two, three".

The boxer watched the white shirt try to lift the man with the gummy leg off the floor again. Again, they sagged back down. The man with the gummy leg did not stop cursing. "Up the camel's arse!"

The dodgy white shirt bastard stood up again. He was still laughing. The boxer did not like what he was seeing. Not one bit. This bloke was playing with them. He was just a weedy, scrawny, thief. The boxer knew he could flog him easily. He had flogged bastards like him before. Yesterday was still a blur but somewhere in the mists of memory he knew he could fight. He had fought in tents, in rings, in pubs, on the streets and in lock ups. Someone must have locked him now. Who were all these men shuffling around? Why were they all so quiet? Why didn't they give the white shirt a damn good flogging?

Another naked man came shuffling into the room dripping wet with a cake of soap stuck in his teeth.

"Hey Merv, this won't do." The white shirt tried to march the man with a cake of soap in his teeth back towards the sound of running water. There was a slippery scuffle. The man with the cake of soap in his teeth kept throwing punches. One of them caught the white shirt hard in the chest. There was a short struggle but the dodgy white shirt was too strong and man-handled the soap eater back towards the sound of running water.

The boxer looked on disapprovingly. That was not how you threw a punch. The soap eater was too mad and scrawny. Who had locked him up with these strangers? Where were the Salvos? Why weren't they in charge? He balled his fists even tighter.

The bloke who was not a Salvo came back in. He gave the man with a gummy leg a frown and then chuckled and went over to make one of the beds. The boxer was seeing red. Something was up. He did not like the look of this bloke at all. He moved his legs around trying to feel the floor. He looked around in anger. Some of the silent shuffling men were getting dressed. Where did they all come from? With an effort he managed to stand up again. He could not stop the shaking. He took a few steps to find his balance. He had to get out. How long had he been here? The fog in his brain wasn't clearing. His head hurt badly. He needed a drink. He needed to get his clothes back and flog whoever had stolen them from him.

The boxer took another step. Why was he feeling so crook? The fog in his brain was too thick to see through. He could not remember yesterday or the day before but he knew he could fight. If he snapped off a punch the thief who had woken him would know all about it. He never stood for a flogging. He used to be strong and hard and afraid of no man. This weedy bloke who had woken him was not wearing a Salvo's uniform. Just one punch would put him on his arse. Just one punch and he wouldn't be playing games anymore.

"Hey Bob, the showers are running. Nice and hot. Time to hop in. I will make your bed. Leave your pyjamas here. Your clothes will be here when you come back." The weedy bloke was looking straight at him.

The white shirt was still smiling. So, he thought it was all a joke. He thought he could lock people away and steal their stuff. He needed to be flogged. The boxer tried shuffling and moving his feet. His body had gone missing but there was strength in his hands and fingers. He was seeing red. He could punch. He was not some old punch-drunk prisoner to be pushed around.

"C'mon Bob, time for a shower." The thief mocked him with his smile.

The boxer snapped. He stopped shaking. He was young again. He was a hard puncher. He launched sideways at the white shirt. The little bastard didn't know what hit him. Both men hit the linoleum hard and began wrestling on the floor. The boxer was enraged. He tried to gouge the little bloke's eyes but the bastard had him in headlock and was yelling out for help. So, he had mates! There other thieves here working together! All the other shuffling men just looked on quietly.

The boxer only saw red. The little bastard was not letting him get a punch in but he was losing his grip. He was still yelling for help when he broke away and stood up. The boxer sprang up too. He was strong, he was a boxer, he was young, he should not be locked up. He started throwing big hay- making punches. Nearly all of them missed. The little bastard would not stand still! He kept on ducking and weaving. The boxer got angrier. He heard doors unlocking and other people rushing in the room. He would take them all down! All the bastards! He would flog them all! He was a boxer!

Suddenly the room was full of men with white shirts. None of them were Salvos. The boxer kept throwing hay-makers. The men in white shirts circled warily. The boxer knew he could flog them all.

Then a woman's voice called his name. "Bob! Bob!"

The way she said it took all the sting out of him. Suddenly she was there; between him and all the bastards in white shirts. She was stout and round with a kind but firm face. There was no fear in her eyes.

"Bob! Bob," she said his name again. "It's okay," she stepped closer, looking him straight in the eye. "No one has taken your clothes. You are safe here now." She waved all the men in white shirts away.

The boxer saw his red rage crumple. He started shaking again. His fists unclenched. He knew where was. It was the way the stout woman said his name, so tender and serious. For a moment the fog cleared. He knew he had lost too many fights. He had drunk down too many sorrows. Somewhere on the streets, in the fight tents, in the rings, in locked rooms and in places filled with merciless fluorescent light his life had gone raw and rancid.

The stout woman reached out and took his big bony hand in hers. Her eyes were kind and unafraid. "It's okay Bob, sometimes we wake up having a bad day." She gave his hurting hand a gentle squeeze.

He knew it then, they had locked him away. Somewhere long ago they had thrown away the key. He was another old shuffling man. All the sting had gone.

He gave the stout woman's hand a squeeze. He did not know who she was but she was kind and tender and he knew he could always trust a Salvo.

16

The Rainbow Man

The woman from the high towers felt insanely stressed. The numbers were not good. The directors would not be happy. Whichever way she looked at it there was no more fat to be cut only flesh and bone. The cash flow had dried. It was no time to go getting warm and fuzzy. Inefficiencies required surgical removal. They would have to re-finance and lose more of the furniture. They were running a corporation not a charity.

All morning she had tried to stretch the pie. Again and again, she had crunched the numbers. She had conducted the interviews. She knew who the 'furniture' was. It was her job to save money not people. She might wax lyrical about 'structural realignments' or 'creative synergies' or 'increasing productive interchanges' but the directors had eyes only for the bottom line. They did not care for wage slaves. All the real money belonged with stocks and property. It was her job to manage the welfare issues and the 'packages'. The directors had the bullets ready. It was her job to fire them.

Normally she powered through her days fuelled on sugar and caffeine. Lunch breaks were for shirkers. Most days she liked her life inside the gleaming towers. She liked power dressing and power walking and the thrill of sealing the deal. She was more than good at her job. She managed the metrics of productivity diligently. At work she was courteous and thoughtful. She remembered colleagues' birthdays and bought them cards. Her staff liked rather than feared her. They thought they were all meeting and exceeding their KPIs. None of them would have thought of her as an economic hit woman. They were still under the illusion that loyalty mattered.

The woman from the high towers put her aching head in her hands hoping no one noticed. All morning it had been coming on; a real kicker! It had to be stress! She needed to get out! She needed air! To see something simple and beautiful. To witness something without monetary significance, like a tree or falling rain or an autumn leaf on the wind. She repressed a wry smile. She had been crunching numbers for too long. She was an actuary in another life. In her high tower world, everything got weighed and valued. Assets came first. Slaves and simple beauty came last.

She was glad the virus had all but emptied the office. Those who came in had their heads down, maximising social distance. It felt lonely and unreal. The florescent lights and the conditioned air felt like it was leaching the life from her bones. It was corona time. Business was no longer usual. Something weightless, invisible and ridiculously small was striking blows against the empire. The politicians and the boffins were worried about how things would snap back to normal.

One crisis pressed upon another. The summer of fire and smoke had not long past with inconvenient portents of doom. Now the cash had stopped flowing. Crowds were queuing for the dole. But the directors did not mind. Every crisis was an economic opportunity. If things snapped then let them snap. They all knew the game.

The thing was not to be the last one standing when the music stopped. They were happy that stocks were rising and wages falling. They liked the reserve bank printing money like it was confetti so they would speculate and buy back their shares and jack up the price. The woman from the high towers knew they were all defying gravity. They were all watching the weather. At the first sign of danger they would sell, sell, sell! Only shabby losers were left holding the baby.

The woman from the high towers knew some of the losers by name. She was cutting deep. The directors had been clear. Besides bonuses, everything else was fair game. A good crisis should not be wasted. Something as messy, viral and unreliable as the human element had to be managed prudently. Sure, people were necessary but robots cost less and did not answer back.

Sometimes she thought she might be turning into a machine herself; power walking all over her own humanity. Despite her calculus she did not share in the director's confidence. The world was snapping but it wasn't back to normal. The music was getting patchy. Soon enough, there would be a mad rush for the chairs. Gravity had a way of pulling people down, even directors. She had to get some air. She grabbed her phone and her jacket and almost ran to the lift. All the way down she wondered if she could leap into a new life. Could she risk it? Sure, she was high up in the tower. Her job was not listed for the cut but she was still just a slave after all. She had to get out! She needed to get still! In the meantime, going for a walk would have to do.

The streets were quieter than she expected. It was a late autumn day and the smell of rain was in the air. The season was turning fast. Winter was close, a grey, confining, cold, Melbourne winter that took marrow from the soul. Foot traffic was down to a trickle. All the eye-sore beggars she never liked seeing had been moved on. The few people out and about warily kept their distance. They walked past frowning; their heads locked to devices. Fear of contagion was in the air. Another lock down was likely. Borders were closed across the land. Everyone was masking up and staying low. The good old days had taken a turn for the worse. She put her head down, vigilant for bio hazards and unwanted sociability, she avoided eye contact and started walking.

She shivered at first but picked up her pace. Soon she was power walking, boots rapping out a sharp rhythm on the asphalt. She liked the busy sound of it and put her head back to take in deeper breaths. The cool air was invigorating. Soon she swung along at rollicking pace. She could feel her stress easing with the blood flow. She was a busy blur flitting past shopfront windows. The noises in her head were receding. Her expensive boots did all the talking; sharp, shiny, loud and purposeful. She was almost normal again until she caught sight of herself checking her phone in one of the shopfront windows.

The sight pulled her up sharp. A wave of disgust hit her in the face like a hard slap. She was a slave! She could see it in her ghostly reflection chasing digital phantoms through endless shades of grey. Somehow, she looked ridiculous in her power walking boots and furious swagger. Just like any other shadow in the street she was chased by deadlines and glued to the sleepless grid. She looked up and saw the tower she worked in all lit up in the gloom. She shook her head. One of her recommendations to the directors was to have less lights on when no one was around. She knew it would not be acted on. Facades were not for questioning. Hers too.

She started walking again but the satisfaction had gone. The stress came back with a vengeance. Her head was aching badly. She made a note to go cold turkey on the caffeine. She pulled her coat in tight against the cold and tried to regain her busyness. She still had her head locked to her phone when she almost shirt-fronted a couple of masked pedestrians. She grunted an apology as she wobbled out of the way. She took an erratic evasive move around an elm tree and stumbled over a beggar man she hadn't seen.

She was too polite to curse but she wanted to. Instead, she mumbled another apology as she stumbled back to stride. She hated seeing beggars. They were human eyesores. They were shysters. They affronted decent people who took responsibility for their lives. They were more than annoying, playing guilt trips, ambushing decent people with their hangdog misery and taking advantage of their goodness with their cultivated dereliction.

She shook her head again as her annoyance grew. It had been a while since she had seen a beggar. She thought the authorities had moved them on. Winter was coming and rough sleepers were being quarantined in hotels. That was good. They were a danger and best to keep the danger at arm's length. Why was this beggar still at large?

She took a backwards glance as she walked on. The beggar man did not seem to have noticed her at all. Or was he a beggar? He looked derelict enough with his long dread locks and unkempt beard. He was a tiny man wrapped up in a big brown coat that looked three sizes too big. He sat on some sort of blanket with both arms extending into the air like he was smiling at the sky. He had a bright home knitted rainbow coloured beanie that also looked three sizes too big for his head. His eyes were closed even as he smiled through his broken teeth. For a moment she thought he was at prayer. She stopped mid-stride. She saw what he was looking at. It was the elm tree. Annoyingly, bewilderingly, he looked strangely happy, arms drawing lazy circles in the rain scented air.

Just then an elm leaf brushed her face as it fell. Like the beggar man she also looked up into the branches of the tree. Suddenly she felt overwhelmed with envy. What did he see that she did not? What secret wonder dispensed him from need and attachment? What was he hiding behind his strange tangled smile? What possible power could an elm tree have to make a beggar seem so free and happy?

It was as if the tree had suddenly appeared. Now it had her full attention. She saw the muted afternoon light play across the smooth branches. She watched as it undressed itself in the cold wind letting go one leaf at a time. It welcomed the nakedness of winter. It was complete. It was rooted and at home in its own skin.

The little man kept looking up lost in some sort of perpetual rapture waving his arms like they were dervishes ready for ascension. Just like the tree he seemed inexplicably happy and at home in his own skin.

It was all she could do not to stare. Eventually she decided he was just a beggar after all. Clearly, he was unplugged from reality and lived in some sort of lost world la la dream land. The only reason he could possibly seem so happy was because he had checked out and left the tab to others. She fought down a wave of disdain and annoyance and tossed the little man a gold coin. She watched it bounce across his blanket and disappear into a drain. The little man nodded and smiled and kept both arms waving in the air.

Annoyed at her own callous charity she turned hard on her heels and marched off. All the power was gone from her walking.

Back at the office the afternoon dragged on. Her headache threatened to mug her motionless. Try as she might she could not get the rainbow man out of her head. She kept seeing the coin roll away. Before days-end there would be more coins and lives rolling out of reach. Once, only days ago it seemed; she thought she was giving more than she took; that she was making the world a better place. Then why did that tumbled down little ruin of a man look so happy? Why?

The day wore on. The directors would not be pleased. She no longer cared. She excused herself, walked back to her car park and got her favourite knitted blanket, the brightly knitted one of many colours her mum had given as a love gift when she first left home.

She hurried back, more a scamper than a power walk.

The rainbow man was still there, hands raised in prayer. When she saw him she smiled and he smiled. She laid her gift and burden down.

A rainbow for a rainbow.

She felt better already.

17

The Young Surfer

It was late; too late to be out and he knew it. The sun was setting. The water was turning dark beneath its glassy surface. The desert twilight was shimmering off the cliffs and the young surfer was out the back all by himself. All he wanted was one last wave. For most of the day he had sat on shore watching the salty locals take on the powerful left hander. The young surfer knew it was a wave for the memory banks. But the locals were not a friendly tribe. They were not known for their sociability. They did not mind dropping in. They were hardened sea dogs with a reputation for inhospitality. The young surfer was a strong water man but thought it was better to wait his turn rather than to get his head punched in. The sun was down by the time the locals had left him to it.

Now it was his chance to sit on the button and wait. All the ocean was his to the distant ends of the earth. He splashed the smooth surface and craned his neck to seek the place where sky and sea fused. It was all his in fluid abundance. So peaceful and still and empty. The beach was empty. The sky was empty. The sea was empty.

It was all his to enjoy. He was the last man dancing. All he had to do was wait.

There was a lull in sets while the shadows lengthened. He kept waiting, fighting the twinge of anxiety niggling beneath his impatience. He paddled a bit and then sat up facing the horizon. Nothing was moving. He waited. It was all so still and peaceful. Too still. Nothing visible was stirring. No breeze ruffled the perfect stillness. Sooner or later the left hander would have to roll in. Just one more wave was all he needed and then he would be shore side safe with mother earth again.

He paddled further, making sure he could take off deep when the barrels came. He had been watching the locals. The best of them knew how to go deep. He reckoned he could go even deeper. The ocean held no fears. The limestone reef was razor sharp and unforgiving but he backed himself... The swell had been pumping. All day he had waited for the dangerous men to leave him to it. He was sick of waiting now.

"C'mon Huey, send me a good set" he prayed his surfer's prayer to the surfers' unreliable God.

Nothing.

Just the desert sky glowing golden pink and grey over the fading cliffs and dark water getting darker. Then his head spun hard. What was that! He snapped his head back again. What had he seen? He squinted, eyes swinging hard as he cross-examined the distance. There had been a momentary shadow, maybe two hundred metres away. Something floating silently or was he seeing things. He paddled a bit more vigorously, deliberately troubling the peaceful water.

"C'mon Huey," he resisted the urge to curse his fickle God as he scanned the horizon. The evening just got quieter.

He sighed and exhaled. Willing the waves to come was not going to work on Huey.

Again, his head snapped hard left. This time there was no mistake. He saw the dorsal fin bisecting the surface, slowly negotiating the cliff line. It was not a dolphin or a seal. The fin was moving slowly, angling close in towards the shore, still a long way off but there was no mistake. It could only be one thing.

Shark!

It was hard to stop his head from spinning. The apex predator was patrolling the twilight shore line. It was looking for twilight snacks and likely was heading his way.

He sucked in a curse. It would be the last time he asked Huey for help. But the fin was all of two hundred metres away and the surf had been so good. The danger didn't feel so close. Surely a wave was coming. Surely, he would get that inside barrel. He was more annoyed than scared. Just one more set and he would be done.

His head kept snapping back and forth.

Nothing!

He slowed his breath. Willing himself to become calm. One wave would do it. One wave and he was safe. The cliffs glowered back in the dusk. He scanned the shore and scanned the horizon. It was clear enough. Unless the shark had turned around, every contour of beach and cliff and reef would lead the predator straight towards him. There was no chance they would avoid each other. Thoughts began bubbling and agitating in his mind. Should he just panic and make a mad scramble for the shore? Or maybe if he stayed calm and just eased himself in ever so quietly. Just one slow breath and paddle at a time. Or maybe the prehistoric monster had other things to do and places to see and all he had to do was wait for Huey to send that wave.

He kept on waiting. The waves weren't coming. He tried to stay calm. He paddled a bit closer to shore. Even a small wave would be nice. He scanned the empty horizon.

Nothing.

Then he froze. This time there was no mistaking what he saw. Shark!

The dorsal fin was slicing through the water like a torpedo; just fifty metres and closing. It had to be one of those great whites coming out of the depths. Time unravelled and began playing tricks. He was only a meal in waiting. He was nothing but meat in the food chain. Nature could not care less. All human graces and privileges were gone. Death and darkness were descending. Life was a set of binary options. Be eaten or not be eaten. On, off, in, out, flight, fight, panic, don't panic, live, die.

He went catatonic, pulled his legs out of the water and sat like a yogi. Time deepened its freeze. For the very first time in his young life he felt the utter and terrible inevitability of his own death. Fear fizzed and rifled through his blood. In-between one breath and another the dorsal fin dipped and disappeared. Death was surging towards him with his name on it. His gut clenched in terror but in another part of his mind he was indignant. How could he suddenly fall to the bottom of the food chain? How could fate suddenly reduce him to shark road kill? How had it come to this? That in the end he was no more important than shrimp or krill or phytoplankton. Not as far as the shark was concerned.

Time was abolished. He waited for an age or a micro moment. He could not tell. He knew how great whites attack. How they rise from underneath. How they hit their prey with terminal impact, breaking the surface in mauling precision. He had seen shots of it. Huge monsters holding some poor seal or dolphin in their maw before crashing back to the depths.

He waited and waited and waited. Time was immobilized. The stillness and the dark mocked him. He had died. He was only seventeen and a half and it was all over. He was dead for sure. Everything he might achieve, everyone he might love and everything he ever had to receive was now shark bait. He was collateral damage paralysed between this world and the next. A temporal warp in the fabric of things opened. Minutes or seconds went by. All that remained was a monster in the depths and his own awaiting death. Whether he raged or wept he was the food. No more important than sea grass.

Time held until the still point snapped and he thrashed his way to the shore in a flurry of pumping panic, and expletives. He wasn't going to give the monster any more chances. If it was him or the shark then he was gambling all his luck on making a screaming paddle for it.

He kept on screaming all the way in. He screamed in terror and rage and relief to be actually still alive. Once back on the beach he lost it completely. He fell headfirst swearing and weeping and grabbing handfuls of sand. The earth had never felt so safe and secure. The great mother was all he ever would need. He wished she might go over and warn that shark. So secure was she on the dry side of the argument. Safe in her protective embrace he could weep freely and watch her finger wag at monsters in the deep. He was later glad that none of the crusty sea dog locals were there to see it. He vowed to never go into the ocean again.

Until the next day.

The sea dogs were back in the water and there was safety in numbers. He figured suffering the locals rage was better than surfing alone.

Back on shore he told one of the old sea dogs about it while they washed sand from their wetsuits. He tried to be cool.

"Fuck man! I saw a shark here yesterday. A real big mother feeder!" he tried hard not to seem too breathless.

"Yeah mate" The old sea dog was unperturbed. "That old boy has been doing the rounds. Seen him here lately. A couple of months ago one chomped a guy's board. Missed him by that much." The sea dog held up two fingers grinning nonchalantly. "Yeah, old whitey just got a mouthful of fibre glass for his trouble. Reckon you might be lucky. He doesn't think surfers taste that good. Might still be picking glass from his teeth."

The young surfer sucked in his fear. He put on a grinning mask of his own. He wasn't letting the old sea dog watch him lose face. The salty local could blow hard all he liked. The universe was different now. His run of luck was up for grabs. He had been warned. He never went surfing after sunset again.

He knew now that he was on borrowed time.

18

The Fire Fighter

On the morning before the fires the air was taut and still. The sledge hammer heat had temporarily retreated. The stripped back hills looked too parred to the bone to burn. Outside his window the pastor saw bits of green still defying the apocalypse. People were still shopping as usual. The talking heads on the radio sounded alert but not alarmed. Should fire demons appear there were strike teams of seasoned fire fighters to strike them down.

'Maybe, just maybe,' the pastor said to himself, 'Maybe we have got this.' He turned up the air conditioning, stayed tuned to the radio and bunkered down. It seemed even when the air was ready to burn the machine must go on. Money was still short, people still needed busloads of faith plus shopping to get by. He saw no reason to cancel the evening service. The day got hot and wore on.

Sometime later the minister went out to check the sky. There was a new hot whispering breeze and the magpies had taken guard on the shady side of the house. The sky was clear but the air felt thin and brittle.

He went inside to listen to the radio again. This time the talking heads didn't sound so calm. The gathering heat was unnerving despite the clear skies. He got on the phone to ring around and cancel church. 'Surely the strike teams will get on top like they always do,' he told himself. 'The strike teams would swing into action and were ready to go. Seasoned fire fighters would keep all the shoppers safe.'

About an hour later he went outside and he knew differently. The rasping breeze was now a Mordor wind; a monster mushroom cloud rose higher than any dark tower he could imagine. The besieging cloud rose vertically towards the stratosphere. The pastor fought down a wave of panic. It looked like all the world was on fire. Moments later the power failed. The afternoon unravelled. Day became night.

Soon the hot, smoke-punished air was filled with the lament of wailing sirens. The long darkness seemed endless. He went outside and tried to wet down the roof unnerved by the constant wail of the sirens. He ran into a sobbing neighbour terrified they would all be burning soon. She was trying to hose down the wall of her house. "I can't take this, I can't take this," she gasped between sobs, dismayed at the lack of water pressure in her hose. "I can't live like this anymore; I've got to get out of here."

He felt exactly the same. He was in a panic. His car was unpacked and he had nowhere to go. Fire demons were devouring the night.

Days later the fires still burned. During that time the pastor hardly slept. When the very first ashen dawn broke, news came in of deaths: So many of them! Too many of them! Some he had known. Some he would soon have to bury. Some others had stories of astonishing near miss, everywhere there were stories of loss and shocked amazement.

Days later the pastor took a back road, dodging police road blocks. Fires were still burning leaving the back road eerily empty and cloaked in thick smoke. It was a long drive back to the parish. The national broadcaster had sought the use of his parish grounds. A bevy of chaplains, experts, responders and officials were all parachuting in.

The long drive gave him time to think. Smoke made the going slow. Trauma was in the air. News of yet another death sat on his phone. Every gnarled and looming eucalypt felt like it had a story to tell. The pastor wondered if they too had survivor's guilt like he did. Or were they still mute with terror and secret understanding?

The air was pregnant with threat but the trees seemed rooted in some deeper place. It felt to the pastor that the trees were reaching out for all the shrivelled, riven, burnt green things in the world and holding silent vigil. He knew there was going to be a lot of vigils and requiems. Why shouldn't the trees have their own?

When he arrived at the parish grounds, the pastor was too tired and numb with dread to feel nervous about the possibility of his fifteen seconds of fame. With luck he might not talk at all. He was a recluse that disaster had smoked out and thrust in front of spotlights and mobile microphones. He watched with detached weariness while technicians adjusted wires and calibrated equipment. A frowning celebrity presenter came across still poring over his notes to thank him for the venue. After a perfunctory hand shake the pastor was left alone. It was only then he noticed fine white particles raining down on his head and shirt. He took a seat next to a volunteer fireman and started to brush the particles from his sleeve.

"Incredible." He said to no one in particular, watching the brushed ash trails on his black t-shirt like they were some form of abstract art, it looked like snow.

"Do you know what that is?" The minister looked at the gaunt and weary fireman sitting next to him. He had blood-shot, sunken-in, hard to read eyes. His fire fighter's overalls were covered in soot and grime. He looked like he had not slept for days. He patted the minister's sleeve and then gestured skywards past the camera lights. "All those embers. They are still falling. It is the remains of fire on your shirt."

"Really," the pastor hadn't been thinking straight for days. "It almost looks like snow."

"Not snow, ash," the fire fighter smiled and shook the pastor's hand. "It has been raining ash ever since the fires." The fire fighter spoke in hushed tones while they waited to go live. The night was balmy and warm. It would have been a perfect late summer's night save for the acrid smell of smoke and the indiscriminate ash.

"Looks like a hard rain falling then," the pastor smiled wanly at his own pun. Both men looked up past the array of cameras.

"Yeah, it was a plasma fire. Never seen anything like it and I used to work for the metropolitan brigade. All those embers were bullets. Like a hurricane of fire. The fire made its own storm. All the way up into the atmosphere. Those embers kept on burning high and now they are still falling days later. Believe me you did not want to be there." The fire fighter spoke softly as he patted the pastor's sleeve absent-mindedly.

"Where were you?" the pastor asked feeling both dread and awe. The fire fighter looked calm and composed but there was something stripped back and unreadable about his eyes. The pastor wondered if he looked the same.

"Marysville. He gave the pastor a hard look.

"Shit!"

"Yeah," the fire fighter nodded. "We were one of the first units in. People were still in their houses pleading for us to save them. We were just a dad's army from a one-horse hamlet. I'm fifty and I was the youngest. All we could do was use siren and speakers to tell people to shelter down at the park. We had to leave people behind. It was crazy. Lots of terrified people begging for us to save them. Thank God if you believe in God." The fire fighter gave the pastor another knowing look. "Thank God we practiced our emergency fire drill just the week before. We had time to set up and take shelter. Believe me, reverend, you didn't want to be there."

"Shit!" the pastor said again, feeling the inadequacy of his expletive. The fire fighter was speaking calmly and softly bellying the look in his eyes. Only a few minutes before the pastor had confirmed notice of another death conformed in Marysville. The whole town had gone and many had died.

"It must have been terrible." The pastor said not knowing what to say.

The fire fighter gave him a long look. "At least we got the screens up and the sprinklers working. It was all we could do."

"Thank God!" the pastor said without much conviction.

The fire fighter shook his head. "Thank dad's army. Those old blokes are true grit. The embers were like tracer bullets. There were gas bottles going off all over town like bombs. It was horrible. Some people say it could have been worse. I don't know if it could have been much worse where we were."

Both men squinted into the television lights. They were about to go live and across the nation.

"Yeah," the pastor decided expletives were useless. "It must have been terrible," he said again. He did not tell the fire fighter that the latest death logged on his phone was from Marysville. An old salty bushman who believed sirens and emergency evacuations were for sissies. His widow no doubt was one of the luckier ones saved by the dad's army. Despite not knowing the bushman, the minister felt overwhelmed by the horror and grief of it all. His imagination had been going to places he tried not to follow.

He gave the fire fighter a long look of his own.

The fire fighter shook his head again and drew in a shallow breath. Clearly words weren't up to the task. The pastor could only wonder how the fire fighter was still standing. Even at just one remove from disaster he could feel the tightness in his chest threatening to shatter and splinter everywhere. Words were dross flying and falling in the raining ash.

It was then the celebrity presenter announced they were ready to roll. Words were back on the menu regardless. All across the nation a word storm rolled. The talking heads were back with a vengeance looking for someone to blame. There was a reckoning to be had about heat waves, fallen power lines, arson, trauma, greenies, lucky escapes, uncommon valour, human kindness and a climate catastrophe whose time had come. Everyone was talking at the speed of light.

The fire fighter and the pastor both had their fifteen seconds of fame. Then they were done. They looked up past the camera lights. They said nothing.

Not a single word could stop the hard rain falling.

19

The Naga Babba

The tourist knew he should have kept his head down. Everyone else did. In the oldest city on earth the locals knew a thing or two about curse and blessing. They knew not to cross a naked *Naga Babba* out and about with the noon day shadows. No one wanted to be singled out for the death stare. They kept custody of their eyes so as not to provoke offence. Despite the tightly packed lane they found room, rolling aside, tucking in shoulder and arm so as to allow the ash covered, butt- naked *sadhu* through. He was like a dreadlocked Moses parting the Red Sea. He was a hash fired, Shiva-marked warning. No one was safe. The destroyer was nigh. No one was going to get out alive. Just one stray look at a man with eyes on fire might be enough to upend the world. In the city of death, the locals knew this. The day of ash was coming. There was no need to hasten it along the way.

The top heavy tourist was not so wary. Curiosity got the better of him. They faced off. One hard glance made the tourist forget his name. It was not a fair fight. The *Naga Babba* locked on. He had nothing to lose and the tourist had everything. All his alibis were up for sale. The *sadhu's* eyes could drill through steel. They took just a nanosecond to find him wanting. He was soft, over-weight and terrified of death. He had evaded life and love and manufactured a thousand excuses for not showing up. All to no avail. He was going to die.

The force of it hit him like a hard slap in the face. The *sadhu's* hash-rimmed eyes were all over the tourist in a blink even without breaking stride. The tourist panicked. He started looking for some shadow in which to hide but it was noon. He wanted to run, to cry, and to shout 'how dare you!' But the sadhu's hard stare pulled him up short. There was no doubting it was entirely personal. It had to be! Never in his entire life had anyone looked at him with such precise hostility. Never had he been so stripped bare and reduced by a single withering glance.

The overheated tourist felt assaulted. He wanted to strike back, to snarl and shout insults. How could it be? That some deranged hash addled loser in the back streets of Varanasi; that some crazed *fakir*; thought he had a right to interrogate his soul? He was too panic blown for answers. He was the one stripped naked. Did the *Naga Babba* have some supernatural gift like some mediaeval saint of old? Could he read souls? Did he do day trips between heaven and hell? What had he seen to make him so implacably rude without saying a word? Did the *Naga Babba* know every squalid detail? Every sin?

The Naga man swayed past like Lord Shiva himself. He was a dancer out of tune with the rest of the world. He was devotee of a hard God, short on tender mercies and easy solicitation. A man with burning eyes who had taken the leap. A man who had stared at death so long he had the ash to prove it. He gave the tourist one more imperious look; just another dismissive appraisal, and was gone. Less than a moment later the crowded street closed in; the locals emerged from the shadows; they knew the danger had passed.

The tourist wasn't so lucky. Despite the heat of the day he felt cold. The *Naga Babba* had stripped away his thin veneer of innocence. He was going to die. He knew that now, even as he tried desperately to forget. He stumbled on, ignoring the merchants hawking for business. The shadows were still shrinking. He had to get to the great river. He had to touch the mother Ganges. He had to ask the question now that death was guaranteed. Was life meaningless? Did he have some purpose in the bigger scheme of things? Should he take the leap? Could he take the leap? Be a pilgrim instead of a tourist?

By the time the tourist reached the mile wide river he was out of breath and his head was spinning. The hot sun punched through the smoke of the funeral pyres. The stench of it nearly made him gag. Chastened, he stumbled away from the circling dogs and the funeral *wallahs* seeking clearer light. Loudspeakers were broadcasting competing creeds. Old yogis chanted mantras battling with *muezzins* calling the faithful to prayer. Hippies were doing tai chi and fat pilgrims were doing their ablutions. Only the river was silent.

For a long while the tourist sat considering the cost of being a pilgrim. He was still wondering when the shadows lengthened and the lazy sun sank into a dust strewn sky. The river rolled on, carrying lighted candles, barges, tourist boats and human remains.

'You too', it felt like a promise. 'You too are on your way to the ocean refusing no river'. The tourist nodded in agreement. Silence felt better than words. Like the river, he was in no hurry to get there. The sun was approaching the end of the day and he was done wondering. Just a few yards away he looked up to see some street boys playing cricket. A little boy was taking guard next to an open drain facing some hostile bowling. Feeling calmer the tourist wandered over to watch. He laughed and said "Hey, how about you pick on someone your own size."

All of a sudden the *Naga Babba* was forgotten.

The boys laughed back at the tourist and circled around. "Which country you from?" they asked in practiced broken English.

"Australia," the tourist announced bravely. He fancied himself with the ball if not the bat.

"Ah!" all the boys chorused. "Alan Border! World cup! Very good. Very good."

"Yes," the tourist beamed back. "World champions." He watched on while the little boy got hit by another bouncer before getting dismissed. "Not fair," the tourist cried. "Let me bowl to one of the big boys."

It was on then. A test match between nations. The biggest boy took the bat and stood his guard. The other boys hovered with glee. There were giggles all round.

The tourist gripped the ball and gave it a spin. He sauntered in to release the ball. He figured the cocky lad would not see his yorker coming. He gave the bowl a twirl and sent it right towards middle stump. An excellent delivery that would have done him proud back home.

The oldest boy was ready. With masterful, wristy Indian finesse he rocked back and cut the ball hard and straight up the guts of the nearby drain.

The tourist looked on dismayed. The lad came down the crease all smiles swinging his bat and holding up two fingers.

"That will be two rupees," he grinned triumphantly.

The tourist laughed harder than the boys.

He knew he was done.

He wasn't naked yet but he was getting there.

20

The Moon Boy

Turning thirteen was not what it was cracked up to be. His parents were liars. They had given him false hope. "Soon," they said, "Soon you will be an adult". They even said it twice; both in his birth day card and on his birth day. The present they gave was not much. Not like the BMX bike his best mate's parents had given. Sure enough, the new swimmers were good and the shirt and pants were appreciated. And, at least they had thrown in some goggles and snorkel with the swimmers but all the same, his parents weren't big on fun. He still had to do the dishes with his annoying little sister. He still had heaps of chores to do after school and pocket money was not an option. He was still forced to do homework. He still had to contend with his mother's iron rule over watching television. They still made him go to bed at eight thirty. They were liars.

His mum was the worst. The television remained off until six o'clock. By then all the good shows had come and gone except for the spooky Doctor Who, which the boy found weird and terrifying. Every time the theme music came on he always felt the same exciting thrill of terror. It was almost his favourite show. Every night if he could, he would turn it on and enter unknown worlds, if his mum let him get away with it. Much of the time she didn't. She was cranky and good at showing it.

"Go and play outside," was her regular command. Other times she would spoil the fun and tut and frown in disapproval. "Haven't you got something better to do?" If that didn't work, she was good at nonverbal communication. It never took much to get her huffing and puffing and slamming doors. Failing that, his mum could always come good with a sermon.

"In my day we had to do a lot more than you. I was not even allowed to read after school until everything was done. In my day...."

Her sermons had limited success. On luckier days he would escape outside and go across the road to watch television with the Spencer boys. They had a good mum. There he was able to watch Batman, Get Smart and Bugs Bunny without his mother frowning.

The worst of it was when his father came home. He was usually in before the seven o'clock news. Every night the boy and his little sister knew to lie low until his father undid a longneck and berated the television. He would always curse and declaim until their mother got a beer of her own and maneuvered their father back to the kitchen. It wasn't easy to move him. It was clear their father thought the world was a mess. From what he saw of the news the boy was beginning to understand why. Perhaps he was not so far from being an adult after all. Every night there was something terrible happening, something terrible to worry about. There was war in Vietnam. The communists looked like they might win. The boy had heard about the Tet offensive and had seen the picture of the napalm girl. She was so small, so anguished, and so melted in pain. The boy couldn't forget her crying face. He had seen the picture of the soldier blowing a man's brains out. It looked so terrible and real; not like the bad guys dying on television. There was war elsewhere too. The world was a mess and just like at school it felt like the bullies were in charge. The seven o'clock news was one television show the boy did not mind missing even if it meant doing the dishes with his little sister.

At school the boy kept out of the way of the bullies by being a library nerd. He loved history and geography and time traveling. Every lunch time he would visit ancient empires, rising and falling. The world was mess then as well and they did not even have television. It did not seem to the boy that human beings were any better at stopping the mess.

His father certainly thought so, which is why Wednesday night was so good. Every Wednesday night his mum's iron rule was subverted. He was allowed to stay up and watch Star Trek with his dad. His mum predictably huffed and puffed while the boy and his dad left the seven o'clock news behind. Television had never been better. Every Wednesday the boy went off world and joined the crew of the Enterprise. On the Enterprise the world was not such mess. The brave Captain Kirk and the brilliant Commander Spock were there to save the day. Science and reason prevailed. No one was worried about the Chinese or the Russians anymore. No one seemed to worry about money or wanted to go to war against other human beings. The humans were the good guys and the Klingons were the bad. The boy was in a hurry to get to the final frontier. On the way he had photon torpedoes and phasors up his sleeve. Somewhere out and beyond little planet earth there were worlds filled with dazzling wonders. Off world was the place to be.

Which is why, like nearly everyone else, the boy was so excited the day the moon landing came around. Star Trek was coming to life!

His maths teacher was in raptures, "This is it, boys and girls. This is humans at their best, stretching their limits and doing what we never thought was possible. Science fiction is coming to life."

The boy nodded fervently even though he was useless at maths. The final frontier was surely in sight!

The classroom was close and stuffy and the little black and white screen felt nearly as far away as the moon. Much of the time the screen was so fuzzy and grainy he couldn't see a thing. It was taking ages to land. He could feel his excitement dropping. They were all taking an awfully long time to get going, not like back on the Enterprise. Before he knew it he was fidgeting and goofing off.

Then all of a sudden the sound was turned up on the television. A ripple of excitement went around the classroom. The boy felt it too. He stopped goofing and strained to see and hear what was happening. He was too amazed to be annoyed by the grainy images. Humans had done it! They had gone off world! Star Trek was possible. They all heard Neil Armstrong say:

"That's one small step for man. One giant leap for mankind."

Later, back in his own class, their maths teacher told them they had seen history in the making. The boy nodded in excitement. The world was not the same. They were all now on their way to the final frontier. Humans were really smart. Anything was possible.

The ride home from school was an anticlimax. The world looked exactly like it always did. History did not seem any different. When he bought some potato cakes from the fish and chip shop the man behind the counter looked as surly as he always did. Out on the streets people were doing what they always did. No one looked excited about history being made. When evening fell he looked up to the sky but the moon was nowhere to be seen. Over at the Spencer boy's house, Bugs Bunny was digging holes for other people to fall into. No one was going off world.

Back home there were chores to do and his mum was cranky. By the time the seven o'clock news was coming around his father was back with a beer in his hand and ready to face down the world. But when the news came on he sat down and stopped his usual cursing.

The boy sat down too and left the dishes to his sister. Together they watched highlights of the moon landing. This time the boy could see more clearly. It was still grainy but it looked like the astronauts were having fun and kicking up moon dust. They had already turned into history. Outside it was dark and overcast. The moon was in hiding.

Then he saw a picture he had never ever seen before. It was just a plain black and white photo taken from the lunar module. But there it was.

Earthrise.

The boy could not take his eyes off it. There it was; his world appearing, just a small slice, rising against the moon's horizon. There was the mess. There was his world where naked girls were set on fire with napalm and prisoners had their brains blown out. There they all were, hanging in the blackness. There they all were, all of them passengers on a fragile world. No longer them and us. No longer! Now; there could only be us!

The boy felt his whole body come alive. He was amazed. He was no longer on the crew of the Enterprise. Now he would be an astronaut in his own mind. He had seen a vision. One that everyone needed to kneel on the moon and see. There it was:

Earthrise.

One world only.

One world belonging to them all.

21

The Soldier's Son

The eulogist was almost done when the realisation hit him. They had already cremated the old man. His father, the trenchant atheist, had requested a private cremation without a funeral or wake. Ever the rebel, the eulogist thought the living not the dead should have the last word. Besides it was only a memorial service and the derelict old catholic church had not seen worshipers in years. The priest was a bit derelict too; one of those old liberals not yet run to ground.

The eulogist was usually good with words. Ever a romantic, he was doing his best to colour his father's life in a 'boys own' mystique. The more he spoke, the more he understood how much he never really knew his father. Over the years both had gone missing on each other. They were both very alike and very different. Both of them were artists and fighters. They both had problems with authority but the eulogist had preferred flight over fight in the greater scheme of things. The old man on the other hand was a warrior through and through. His nine lives and counting felt too big for words.

The more the eulogist tried to speak the more he felt his father was defying description and gravity.

As well as clouds of nostalgic over-kill they were covering all that remained of his father with billowing clouds of incense. The priest was good on the thurible. The dilapidated Catholic Church was transfigured by beams of smoky light shafting through frosted windows in the midwinter sun. A shaft of light was falling directly onto his father's Legionnaire's officer's cap. Just behind the cap was a photo of his father holding a cigar and smiling raffishly in his French foreign legion uniform. His father the atheist, was being outdone by God at the last. The light it seemed, had spoken.

The eulogist kept talking, almost like he would about a stranger. He had so much he wanted to say. His father the man of culture, his father the fine artist, his father the libertine, his father the class deserter, his father the raconteur, his father the restless rebel with a cause. His father the hired man of war. He left out the more ordinary domestic details. He barely mentioned how amazed he was the old man had achieved such a long life. It had to be a dead set miracle.

The eulogist knew he was getting lost in verbal over-kill. He had come without notes but his confidence was floundering. At least he had satisfaction at the sight of his father's photograph haloed in winter light. The old man had zero liking for the Catholic Church. Nearly being put to death by Franco's fascist Catholics had left a lifelong distaste for the institution although he did profess a liking for Cistercian beer and a fondness for certain 'good catholic girls'. The eulogist figured his father wouldn't mind the priest. At least he wasn't one of those sharp and pointy right wingers so garden-variety common throughout the franchise.

The eulogist could see that the small crew of friends and mourners he had invited to the memorial were losing focus. Presumably, none of them could quite believe the old bastard had inhabited so many incarnations. Neither could he. He knew something really important was getting lost in translation. The man in uniform with movie star good looks was disappearing in a cloud of incense smoke and tall stories.

The eulogist was trying hard not to turn his father's life into a ripping yarn about a man he hardly knew. The more he talked the more immaterial his father became. He kept painting word pictures of all the nine lives and counting. He poured the romance on thick.

The first life of a privileged Brighton school boy was a mere biographical footnote. Going to university to study architecture before running off to Europe was when it got more interesting. The eulogist was passionate about how his father brawled on the streets with workers against union busting thugs. That was when the old man deserted his class. Out of the blue he became an angry socialist. It was the nineteen twenties and the world was in post war convulsion. Old empires had fallen and a roaring new one was about to tear itself apart. By the time the nineteen thirties came around his father had joined the international brigade fighting alongside George Orwell against Franco's catholic fascists. A daring jail break saved him from the noose and he disappeared into Africa with the French foreign legion. Years later some British airmen helped him desert back to Britain. There he signed on as a merchant crewman on the Atlantic convoys. Later, once they regularised his papers, he enlisted in the army and was part of D Day. It was the only war that his father never talked about.

The eulogist was just up to talking about the decline and fall of his father into feral isolation and happy substance abuse. Even the end had to be romantic. When he got back to Australia they arrested him on suspicion he was an alien. The boy from Brighton had disappeared from the records and had to be fast talked back to life. Afterwards life was never so heroically interesting. The eulogist barely mentioned domestic life or how his mother did so much of the heavy lifting. The returned soldier became a commercial artist and a reluctant family man. The best thing about life in the suburbs was getting out of them. The end years away from the maddening crowds living amongst the ferns and the mosquitoes on the shady side of the Otway's was just another biographical footnote.

Not before time, the priest caught the eulogist's eye and gave him the wind up signal. The eulogist had segued to Voltaire and was trying to say something witty about God having the last laugh. He knew his Francophile father would have approved. Ever the Marxist, his father had no problem with religion being an opiate. So long as the ruling classes did not oppress the masses with it which of course they always did. But the reference was lost on the dazed mourners. The priest intervened:

"Hey, how about we give Voltaire the last word. You know what he said on his death bed when he was asked to renounce the devil. 'Now is not the time to go making enemies.' Same goes for God"

Everybody chuckled.

So did the eulogist.

Silence beckoned. A strange unexpected memory interrupted his flow. It was like his father had stepped out of the incense. Suddenly he was no longer distant. Only a few weeks before his father's death they had walked the block together. The old man wanted to get rid of rabbits. He hobbled along on his stick with the old rifle they had not convinced him to get rid of. The old man was determined to wreak vengeance on the rabbits raiding his vegie garden. The moment one of the flighty creatures showed up was a revelation. It was a deadly ambush. The old man let go of his stick and dropped to his knee with a fluency of movement defying his years. With practiced expertise he took aim, held still, and fired. The rabbit was taken with a single neat headshot.

It was then the eulogist realised who he was. He suddenly saw all those old war stories coming to life. The fog of war had cleared. The old man was gone and now another man he did not know took aim and fired. The eulogist could see him now. He was the son of a killer, a mercenary, a soldier of fortune, a raging wounded warrior who never came home.

The eulogist finished talking and looked to the priest. They had not been able to find a text suitable for his Marxist atheist father. Nothing in the good book seemed to come near. It appeared Voltaire might have conquered after all but on the spot the priest suggested a short verse, seeing they were inside a church, even a dilapidated one. He gave it to the eulogist to read.

'*Foxes have holes and the birds of the air have nests, but the Son of Man has nowhere to lay his head.*'

The eulogist didn't think it said enough. Neither did the priest. It was a spur of the moment thing. Jesus sometimes had trouble being definitive but maybe one struggle held another.

They all grew silent. The midwinter sun transfigured the air. It was okay.

The light had spoken.

22

The Control Freak

The son was in no doubt, it was lockdown, not COVID that was killing his mother. Her dementia had taken off like wildfire ever since bureaucrats had incarcerated her along with his father. Visits to the nursing home were always difficult. Now they were agony. He had to brace himself every time. His mother could not understand why they now talked through plate glass. Her look of sheer desperation speared him every time. Dementia was cruel. Instead of the cheeky, playful, beautiful woman he had known, his mum was reduced to a weeping child. Instead of the strong open-hearted woman he had confided in, she was a crumpled wreck disintegrating rapidly before his eyes. Day by day she got worse. Only once she became bed ridden did the control freak of a manager make concessions. The nurses were saying his mother had days not weeks. Now she was allowed one visitor at a time, for thirty minutes only, so long as they jumped hoops and wrapped themselves in PPE.

The manager made the new palliative care arrangement sound like a generous allowance. It made the son's blood boil. It was hatred at first sight. Why did such unctuous patronizing control freaks do so well in this world? The manager did not stop smiling as he outlined policy. He glowed with positivity as he held the right note of concern. Phrases like pastoral care and resident welfare rolled easily off his tongue. The son could only nod grimly and resist the urge to slap the manager in the face. He knew a corporate arse coverer when he saw one.

"Yes, I know this is a very difficult time for all the family." The manager was not unsympathetic. "But we have a duty of care to all our residents. I am sure you understand." The manager sounded supremely reasonable. It made the son even angrier. He knew management speak when he heard it. Every dot point was tied down and he would have to obey one way or another. Image must trump substance every time.

It reminded the son of the front entrance to the nursing home. It was neatly anodyne and pleasantly beige with lots of air brushed brochures advertising retirement nirvana. They made the whole establishment sound like it existed solely for the most altruistic of purposes. Colour saturated photos of contented seniors stared from every page. The glowing blurbs gushed about care and ease of days but beneath the spin, the son knew that the real pastoral care was being done for board room directors and cashed up shareholders. Warehousing decrepit elders with substandard care was good business. None of the profiteers felt a single bat squeak of care for his poor incarcerated parents, especially the manager.

The son thought of the manager as the worst sort of bureaucrat. The sort good at kissing up and kicking down. It made his mood sour. The world had lots of scarcity but not of bureaucrats. There were control freaks everywhere. Just like the manager. Everywhere you looked they were moving up the greasy pole. The further up you went, the worse it got. They were in government, in medicine, in business, in churches, in the military, in the police and up and down the corporate state. They were all kissing up and kicking down.

The son did not doubt the rank-and-file staff were doing their best to care for his mother. Getting past the manager without wanting to do violence was the tricky part. As he came up the drive and entered the foyer he hoped to be spared. He wasn't. The manger met him with a practiced smile and another word about policy. The son tried to keep his face calm. The man always seemed so apparently sincere and so apparently pastoral. How he hated that word pastoral. Whose idea was it anyway? Were human beings just helpless sheep needing well paid shepherds? Was his mother just a mad ewe ripe for the culling? Sure, lots of churchy middlemen had dined out on the role over the centuries but these corporate spin merchants were another thing entirely.

Once more the well-oiled manager gave the son a lecture about PPE. He was at pains to see the son understood. "Care must not be compromised," the manager advised with an easy smile. He gave the son an appreciative pat. "Have a nice visit," he said, with a smile too lazy for his eyes.

The son wanted to murder him. There was nothing nice about his mother's slow-motion ruin. His sourness deepened. His thoughts were black. It struck him that there was nothing like a visit to a nursing home to say his culture was in terminal decline. No! That was too mild an opinion. More likely civilization itself was in its death throes. How was it that unctuous and disingenuous power trippers like the manager got paid so handsomely while shit kicking rank and file staff who did all the arse wiping, back breaking work got scandalously low wages? It meant only one thing. His culture was sick to its core. His culture despised the aged and removed them from sight. To be elderly was to be contemptible. They were eyesores. He fumed and fulminated until a twang of guilt pulled him up short. Everyone in his family was in on the nursing home decision. They all insisted the time for advanced care had come. No one had said anything about incarceration or a death sentence.

None of that stopped him loathing the manager. He represented the controlling status quo his parents had laboured under all their lives. The pyramid system. They were the little people on the bottom.

How did the powers and principalities find willing minions to kick down and kiss up? How did they hold onto power? They could always persuade stupid people to act against their own interests. There were always control freaks for hire. There were always eager sycophants and enforcers ready to feel inflated and secure. Mostly they came from the defective sex. All through history young men were cannon fodder but they were also easily recruited to the idea of trickle-down glory. Oppressors got no end of support from willing and angry young men. It seemed there were always men eager to be seduced by power. The powers and principalities were good at finding skilled managers to keep the cannon fodder coming. They usually directed the action from the rear of battle lines. No empire or fascist power or tin pot tyrant could exist without a cadre of amenable managers. They needed control freaks in case the slaves got out of hand.

The son saw it all happening in the nursing home. The staff at the bottom were part of a neo feudal corporate system. They were expendable and easily commodifiable just like their elderly charges. They were captured and held to ransom by the manager and his over lords.

Once he got inside the son did his best to smile at the staff. With the lockdown in place the halls were empty. Staff looked tense and tired. Getting through the main open living area nearly brought him undone. It was early November and the glitz and detritus of the season was plastered everywhere. No residents could be seen but Santa and Rudolf were running amok. It felt like the residents had been replaced by reindeers. The sight wiped the smile back off the son's face. His mood soured again. He wanted to go bare knuckled with every Santa he saw. He kept his head down and hurried to the room where his mother was.

When he got to his mum's room, his dad was sitting by her side half asleep. One look told him his mum was dying. The sight took his breath away. She was on a low bed, unconscious, lying prone with her mouth open. It looked like any breath would be her last. He flinched and caught his breath. It was hard to recognize this was the same life filed, love filled woman who had nurtured him so much and so often.

"Hi, Dad," he put on a bright face for his father.

"Ah! Hi, Son," his fathered brightened visibly on seeing him.

His father's chair was close enough to reach his wife's shoulder and face. They said nothing while his dad fished for his hearing aids. The son tore his PPE off, went to the other side of the bed and took his mother's hand. It felt limp and cold, like she was already half way out of her body. They said nothing. He gave his dad a long look. His father looked tired but somehow relaxed; as if his wife's dying was just another natural part of their life together. The son wondered if his father really knew what was going on.

"It won't be long, Dad," he said after a while, praying it would be so.

"Yes."

His dad smiled calmly. His son tried to hide his frown. Did his dad really not get it?

He decided to concentrate on his mother. He gave her hand a gentle squeeze and started talking as if she could hear everything he was saying. He started talking about the family that had gone before. He lingered slowly over the litany of the departed. Occasionally he segued into an anecdote and at the end he assured his mother that she too would be with them all in heaven. He didn't really believe a single thing he was saying but wished he did. Death left so much silence and so much absence. He kept on talking like he did not have a doubt in the world. Death was just a door and eternal vistas beckoned. He really didn't believe it. Death was final. He gave his mum's hand a gentle squeeze. She already looked worlds away.

From the corner of his eye he saw his father staring at him quizzically, head tilted to one side. The son smiled sheepishly. "Um… they say that hearing is the last thing to go. I mean… so even though she seems well out of it, she may still be able to hear."

His father frowned. "What? So she can hear us, now?"

"Yeah. You can talk to her, Dad. Tell her anything you want to say."

His father took a deep breath as he stared at his wife for a long moment. Then he reached across and playfully pinched her nose with a cheeky smile on his face.

"Hey," his father almost shouted. "Hey, wake up sleepy head. You've got a visitor. Don't be so rude!" His father laughed with a broad smile that stopped the son in his tracks. His father looked suddenly years younger. He watched in awe as his father stroked his mother's face in a communion that needed no response from her.

In that moment the nursing home room was filled with light. The son was lucky to get a sideways glimpse of rare beauty. It was a transfiguration. The light was big enough for lifetimes. Some beauties he knew were not even skin deep. He had seen cosmetic confections not worth a nanosecond worth of attention. But he had seen nothing like this! The light went everywhere and the beauty all the way down to the bone. His sour angry mood was gone.

The control freak was gone.

Neither were a match for love. They held no dominion in such light. Now or ever.

23

The Unlikely Missionaries

The unlikely missionaries had wind in their sails. It was all of their own making. They were young and refused to allow a lack of experience get in the road of an abundance of opinion. They believed they were called to save the world.

They were an odd couple. One was tidy and the other was untidy. They thought it as a winning combination. They believed the messiah was short on for hands and needed assistance. They were quite humble about it.

The tidy missionary believed he was called to be a humble priest. Nothing more or less than another Christ manfully manifesting the Most High in season and out. The city of God was in disorder. He would make up for divine fatigue. The walls of the New Jerusalem would be rebuilt and defended. Seized by divine mandate, he would man the watch towers and preach the gospel unfailingly. It was not a time for shirkers and laggards. God's frozen people had to get chosen again. They needed prophets and saints to rouse them from their neurotic stupor. The times called for muscular believing. Slip shod measures could not be tolerated. He had a divine mandate. Sure enough, he wasn't perfect. There were some finishing touches required. Goodness was hard work and perfection a tad difficult. No matter, he was called and chosen. God's city was in trouble and he was on his way.

The untidy missionary felt called to be a humble politician. He would go to the city of the world and manfully ferment nothing less than a spiritual revolution. He had a sharp eye. The world needed rebuilding from the ground up. The old wine skin of the status quo was done. Someone had to take an axe to the corrupt ruling order. Someone had to sow ferment. The world needed revolutionaries with steel in their bones. Sure enough, he wasn't perfect. He still needed a bit more steel. He wasn't quite galvanized. No matter, he was ready to swing the axe. The world needed a third testament even if he had to write it himself. Perhaps he would become a revolutionary legend. Whatever, God was in need of assistance and he was on his way.

The unlikely missionaries brooked no doubts about their call. At least not to each other. Although they were oddly matched they found vigorous accord as they diagnosed the ills of the world. They urged each other to get well ahead of the prophetic curve. There would be no easy accommodation with mammon. They would not be prisoners to comfort. Not for them some craven acquiescence to a corrupt capitalist culture in downfall or a moribund church in decline. Compromises were for weaklings.

The untidy missionary thought that like John the Baptist he would cut hard. Someone sure had to swing that axe. Not for real trees mind you. These he loved as was befitting a man of his greened sophistication. He had a big sticker reading SAVE THE TREES on the back of his car to prove it. Capitalism was a cancer threatening all green things in the world. What was needed were *agents provocateurs*. Just like himself. Someone willing to warn the world about the biblical scale of the disasters that threatened. The world needed a new politics powerful enough to win the battle for hearts and minds in the contest of ideas. The world needed winsome men and good orators like himself. A revolutionary with nerve, entering the halls of power like a fifth columnist cheerfully subverting the ruling agendas. How hard could that be?

The tidy missionary assured the untidy missionary that they had faith to spare. Together they would strike blows against the empire. How hard could it be? No mouthing of formulas would suffice. The missionaries agreed. The city of God and the city of the world were ripe for revolution. Soon a grand new world would rise from the old.

But first they needed a holiday.

A bright sun blessed the day of their leave taking. They set sail and headed east. They would be brothers on the road, boldly seeking solidarity for the manly tasks awaiting. They would travel the road in a beaten-up little Chrysler in keeping with their humility. They felt no need to plan. The road would be their guide. In the mean time they would drive, walk, hike and swim as they philosophised and reconnoitred the cultural landscape like men with a mission.

They were quite pleased with themselves until they met the first headwinds of adversity in a logging town. The world outside the suburbs proved disconcerting. They knew something was wrong when the lady at the sandwich shop met them with a snarl. Outside the shop there were lots of cars and utes with big buffalo stickers on the back. There were no stickers saying SAVE THE TREES but lots of stickers saying SAVE ENERGY BURN A GREENIE TODAY. Suddenly they noticed all the hard looks. They kept their heads down and ate quickly.

The lady at the petrol station was openly hostile. The untidy missionary wished he had chosen some other sticker. The lady was big and butch and came out of her office scowling. She might have been the sandwich shop lady's older sister. She gave them both a hard sneer and then gave the little green Chrysler a solid kick.

"Shit car! You aren't fuckin greenies are ya?"

Suddenly the two missionaries realized their courage wasn't what they thought. They cowered as she stood outside the vehicle cursing.

"Well then, are ya gonna flip the fuel cap switch or do I have to open it with a fuckin sledge hammer?"

They slunk into their seats as she stomped about with bowser pump in hand. They were "fuckin greenies" ripe for burning. Clearly logging towns had different civic codes to the suburbs. They were no match for her. They could see petrol flowing and their car burning. It was a relief to see the petrol go in the tank, pay their ransom and to flee.

It took a few miles before they began to feel manly again. They were shaken but soon started to feel superior. Obviously, the town had gone over to the dark side. They were all hicks, hoons, goons and rednecks. How dare that butch mistake of a woman kick their humble car? They did not need buffalo horns or some muscle car to prove their potency. Soon enough they shook the dust from their feet and settled back into mutual admiration. Not for them any petrol headed need for speed. They were subversives, going slow, smelling the eucalypts, and marvelling at all green things. They were visionaries looking for the Garden of Eden which, unlike those rednecks back in town they were alert for everywhere.

Just as they were rhapsodized the creator's intelligent designs one of the creator's mistakes unfortunately smashed right into them. It looked like some super bug, half the size of a football. It was a mutant horror. It hit the side mirror and burst through the open driver's side window shattering their reverie and splashing green slime everywhere. It wasn't quite the greening they were rhapsodizing.

Suddenly there were shrill cries and unmanly screams as the missionaries reckoned with a grave mistake in the evolutionary chain of being. The untidy one was white with shock as he wiped the slime from his face. The tidy missionary was still screaming as he attacked the remains of the creature with a flurry of panicked blows with his glass drink bottle and then tossed it out the window bottle and all. He watched it explode directly in front of the car travelling behind them.

Again, they panicked. What if the car was from the logging town? What if they were followed? What if they were destroyed by red neck road rage and found themselves saving energy the burnt hard way? The world outside the suburbs was far too dangerous. Courage failed as they made the little green car go as fast as it could. It was quite some time before they calmed down.

So it was that as they came to a town with a broad river, the tidy missionary said they should stop and wash off all their consternation. He waxed lyrical about water as a sacrament with which they would remove the trauma of the day and how the ocean and the river were one. So too were they, as they swam in manful solidarity. How good would it be to brave the crossing together?

The tidy missionary and the untidy missionary were not well matched in lots of ways. One was swimming. The untidy missionary annoyed the tidy missionary with his dog paddle dawdle. About halfway across the tidy missionary stopped thinking about solidarity. The water was black. It was black tea black and blacker still. The river was cold and deep and dark. Unknown horrors were lurking. There might be bull sharks or monstrous bunyips. He decided to save himself.

Their solidarity was a bit wanting.

The next day they made a better fist of it. A new sunrise was full of promise. They marvelled at how well they were marvelling. They left the coast and drove to a lake town in the mountains. They made camp. The untidy one broke out his guitar whilst the tidy one cooked. The untidy missionary was not ashamed to sing out loud.

"Now listen!"

He was doing the eagle rock. It was his one and only song. Oh, how he sang.

"Now listen!"

Oh, how together they would rock the world.

Next door two young girls were camping. They listened and made eyes at the two missionaries. They were nurses on holidays. The untidy missionary grew bolder with his singing. All the day long he made it his mantra.

"Now listen!"

A bit later they all decided to hire a boat and get closer to creation. Storms were brewing but they were daringly manly. So it went. The girls kept making eyes. The tidy missionary was wondering if God had other plans after all.

All was well as they navigated the still waters until another of the creator's mistakes struck. The untidy missionary was leaning back admiring his winsomeness when sudden pain speared his manhood. He did well to take it like a man. The second attack he did not take so well. Suddenly the boat rocked with his screams. There was nowhere to look as he tore off his swimmers and clawed at his testicles frantically. "It's a tick! A tick! Tick! Tick!"

"It wasn't quite the eagle rock.

The girls, being nurses, took it rather well. The tidy missionary adverted his gaze and snapped an oar lock as the boat rocked. Across the lake a high mountain thunder storm was approaching. He panicked and rowed them around in circles. The girls stopped making eyes.

The tidy missionary saw it then. A life of surprises, setbacks and reversals beckoned. He kept paddling in circles and going nowhere. The boat kept rocking. The storm kept rolling towards them. One of the girls being a good swimmer jumped overboard and helped pull them slowly back to the shore.

The untidy missionary saw it too. The revolution was going to be harder than he thought. The creator might have a few more tricks and mistakes up his sleeve. A life of disappointments, compromises and setbacks beckoned. He might not be quite as winsome as he thought.

The next day the girls were well gone. So was the holiday.

As for their mission?

The creator needed to get his act together.

24

The Hairy Hand

He was late for work when it happened. The plumber should have gone ages ago. Most mornings he was out the door and well gone before the predawn light parted the darkness. Business was a monster that kept booming. He was doing well. Plumbers could demand their own price. Customers had to take tickets and wait in line. He was an essential service available only at a premium.

It was such a fine day. Not the sort of day to expect to get bushwhacked by the hairy hand of God. He hated sharp blue sky mornings now, nearly as much as he hated himself.

He worked hard but he knew his wife worked harder. He had a reputation for being a good tradesman. He was easy going, reliable, skilled and careful. Life was full and busy and dollars came in thick and fast. But he knew his unpaid wife had the heavy end of the log. Her pregnancy had been hard. The post-natal time had been harder. Mastitis ripped her confidence apart after it put an end to breast feeding. With her career on hold, a terrible sense of failure nearly submerged her permanently. She put on a lot of weight and got battered by depression.

Most days she put on game face. Some days she even seemed buoyant but he knew her better. She had a good game face but there was a dark shadow not far from the surface. It seemed an age before she began to emerge from the shadows. But time is a healer. After two years his wife was coming back to herself. The haunted sadness still lingered, threatening to submerge her entirely but she held it back with a strength he found amazing.

Getting their baby girl to sleep had been nightmarishly difficult. He tried to get up as much as she did to give her rest but she always did the night watch. She knew he was tired too. So much was happening. He had to work long hours. Now they had the new house, new mortgage, new garden, new car, new business and new child. Life was getting better. It had been a hard haul but the shadows were receding. Little by little his wife's eyes were coming back to life again. They had broken through the ground hog days with a little holiday. Now he was getting on top of the avalanching demand. Now they really were building a new life together just like they dreamed. On top of it all his wife was pregnant again. Now they really would be a family. Now he really was happy. It was as good a reason as any to be running late for once and give the finger to the clock.

That bright morning before dawn he made his wife coffee and then breakfast. Next he got his daughter up, dressed her and put her in the pram so they could go for a vigorous walk with the dog. It was a glorious spring morning. It seemed so wrong to be anxiously watching the clock when the new day was so bright. The season was shape shifting before his eyes with bloom and colour. His little princess was up for adventure sitting up in her pram like a queen, her bright eyes drinking in the world.

It was when they got back that the hairy hand struck. It took only a few stray moments. The clock was not to be denied. Just when he needed to get a move on some evil angel removed his car keys. He was getting very late. Cross and flustered he stomped around cursing himself. As anxiety mounted, he started running around in circles banging in and out the front door, blaming the dog and blaming himself. Then he remembered they were in the tool box in the back of the ute. He ran out, got them and ran back in to get his wallet and say good bye to his wife. Instead of the customary kiss he yelled a farewell and sprinted back to his car. The clock was an unkind master. He threw the ute into reverse and put his foot down.

It was then he heard a dull thud and felt the vehicle lurch and bump. Surprised, he jumped out to check the drive way. Then the world gave way.

He saw before knowing and he knew before he saw. His little toddler baby girl had tottered outside in between the banging of doors and got herself under the wheels. Her tiny little body did not make a move or sound.

He screamed and groaned and fell to his knees searching desperately for signs of life.

"Oh God! No! Oh God no! Oh God! Oh God Oh God! Oh God!"

In between sobs and shouts he tried to do mouth to mouth. His princess, his baby girl was limp in his hands. Somewhere he heard someone screaming. He didn't know who it was. His wife was now with him on the ground. She was screaming and so was he. Together they twisted on the ground beside the limp body of their girl. The bright spring morning now mocked him. The hairy hand had fallen making a mockery of the day, making a mockery of his life. His wife was pleading for him to say she was okay. He could not speak. The hospital was down the road. He drove like a demon. He was the demon. But it was too late.

Afterwards everybody tried to be understanding and supportive. He did not speak. He was alone.

His poor crushed wife dared to say she forgave him. She said it was just a terrible accident. But he knew differently. He had invited the hairy hand to strike. He was the callous demon with no regard for safety. There was no telling how deep the shadows were now. The light had been stolen from her eyes.

His wife kept on saying that she forgave him and he kept on not speaking. He was the demon. Even if she forgave him he would not and could not forgive himself. He was alone.

Everyone else also said it was an accident. They all tried to comfort him. They told him how well he was doing. They circled him with care and attention. He did not speak. He was alone. No one else had been there but him. He did not forget her crushed body and his heart in a million shreds.

The priest had the same difficulty looking him in the eye that everyone else had. He joined the circle of silent witnesses sharing stunned glances. The priest had nothing at all to say about the hairy hand of God.

They did the funeral. The priest was kind. He told everyone God was love and that even if God didn't exist they had to keep on loving. Later on he still did not look him in the eye. The rest of the day was a blur except for how white the little coffin was against all the funereal black and his wife's grip clawing his side. He did not speak. He could not speak. He was alone.

He did not weep. The abyss was too deep for tears. A hard raging numbness was all he had to fall back on. The black earth rose up to meet the bright vessel to complete the darkness. He wanted to join it but with his wife still clawing his side they lurched on.

So did life.

He knew well enough now that the hairy hand was at play and it never played fair. He almost considered if he should become a true believer. He did not claim an interest in theology but figured the hairy hand must have been one of God's mistakes. He was not an educated man or prone to philosophical investigation but didn't think it was that hard to demonstrate essential truths. Life was hard and fey and hairy and just like himself, not to be trusted.

Judging by what the priest said, being a true believer did not matter that much. God's existence was not really a question that mattered. His own was intolerable. Their families circled the wagons. They sold the new house in a hurry and moved to a different town. Summer followed spring and autumn followed summer. His wife gave birth to a baby boy. Bit by bit some light came back to her eyes. She was stronger than he was. He tried to stay with her but he was still alone.

Going back to work and being reliable was now his drug of choice. Even when all the evil angels stripped him of sleep and wracked his heart with bitter accusation he pressed on. Work was what he lived for. Work was his protest against the hairy hand. He would not spare himself. Whatever else he did, he would punish himself to keep his baby boy and wife safe from the dark. Work was a wall to keep the world at bay. He knew it wasn't high enough. Not if it was struck by the hairy hand.

A year went by and then others. He kept working hard and putting on a brave face.

The worst of it were the anniversaries. Every time both he and his wife fell apart. Every time he relived in acute refined detail that bright cruel day. Every time they would crumple. Every time his wife came out of the shadows before he did. Life lurched on.

A few years later he was doing a job for the local caravan park when he saw a familiar face. A man came out of the reception office and barged right into him.

"Gosh, I'm sorry, didn't see you there."

The plumber drew in a deep breath. It was the priest. He looked older and more bedraggled than the plumber could remember as if he had gone to seed. Yet again the priest did not look him in the eye.

The plumber thought he might as well smile and be polite. He extended his hand.

"Hello, Father, it's good to see you. How are you?"

The bedraggled priest looked startled. His brow was furrowed.

"What? Sorry. Do I know you?" he smiled vaguely.

The plumber held on to a thin smile and shrugged. A huge wave of sad recrimination rose up inside. It felt fitting to be forgotten, to be a discarded memory, to be professionally deleted and excised from the world. It was only justice. The plumber kept talking all the same.

"You remember," he attempted to keep smiling, "The funeral."

Suddenly the priest looked stunned. He gaped as the penny dropped. This time he looked the plumber in the eye.

"I am so sorry, so sorry," he blurted quickly, his face colouring with embarrassment. "Please forgive me." He patted the plumber awkwardly on his back. "God! I am so sorry."

"No worries, Father." The plumber returned the pat. There was a look about the priest the plumber knew too well. He looked hollowed out and off balance. Like he also had gone more than a round or two with the hairy hand. He had red eyes and looked weary, like he was on the run from life.

The plumber patted the priest again. It was easy to forgive someone else. "No worries," he said again and kept smiling politely.

"No, no. Please forgive me." The priest blurted again and reached for the plumber's hand. There was an awkward silence.

The plumber smiled wanly. It was not so hard outsourcing absolution. The priest looked ashen and lopsided. It made the plumber feel sorry for him.

"No worries," the plumber shook the priest's hand. It was time to go home and forget about being forgotten. He looked the priest in the eye and patted him again. Absolution done.

The two men exchanged cards and fleeting pleasantries and then went their way.

The plumber went home to his wife.

"Sorry I'm late," he said

"No worries," she gave him an airy smile. "I forgive you."

His little boy was there with shining eyes. "Me too, me too," he giggled waving his arms.

The plumber picked him up and laughed.

"Do you now?" For just a moment he choked and wiped away a tear. "Then that's is all that matters."

25

The Lone Camper

The lone camper had lots of good will towards humanity, it was only people he found difficult. Especially in peak hour. He could not believe the traffic. Escaping from the city was death defying. The peak hour hustle was itchy with tension. Huge behemoths rolled past at terminal velocity. They sat menacingly on his bumper, pushing the world towards deadline fever. Angry tradies in four wheel drives danced in agitation between the lanes. The stop-start traffic was nerve jangling.

He could not see a single person in all the march of glass and steel. The peak hour belonged to the machines. After nearly an hour of going slowly nowhere, he felt tight and coiled with tension. The suburban sprawl was endless. Further out the sprawl felt even more desolate. All the world seemed paved. New estates obliterated the living space between homes. Nature was banished in a sea of black roofs and pre-fabricated concrete. The lone camper grimaced at the sight of so much cheek on jowl dormitory living that only a developer could love.

The road east was not familiar. He had never been to the cape before. He had not reckoned the flight from the city could be so stressful. About an hour or so later he came to the coal valley. Power stations belching smoke made the grey sky match his mood. Further east the country dried out quickly. He felt tired but pushed on. Pale green paddocks gave way to brown ones, littered with dead and dying trees. The remaining green appeared to have departed into weedy exile. Here and there clumps of gum trees defended themselves against the bleaching air. They straggled and hugged each other in defiance of the rainless sky. The land felt threadbare and listless.

Further on the road narrowed. When he crossed the Snowy River he was relieved to see stunted grasslands give way to forest country. The larger trees hid the drought away in shadows and dappled light. He breathed easier. He ignored the dry and pushed on past his fatigue. A little further east he turned left and left the bitumen behind. He could taste and feel the ocean in the air. There wasn't another car between himself and the ranger's office. He breathed easier. Humanity was wonderful after all.

The Khaki clad ranger was avuncular. She chatted and smiled as she handed out maps. "You've come at the best time," she said. "No one here but some grey nomads. Camp where you like."

The day got much better after that. The lone camper couldn't believe his luck. The camp ground was empty and it was spring. The cape was his to explore. He made camp in a ring of banksia trees. He pitched his tent and went to pay homage to the ocean. He had a surf and had enough time to catch the granite headlands glistening ochre bright in the setting sun. Back at camp he lit a fire, and savoured the unfamiliar sand between his toes. He crunched around lightly and ate the wraps he had brought in his Esky.

The November air was balmy and briny. The night closed in.

Possums came out to investigate and quarrel in the fire-light. He opened a bottle of red and tried to listen. The ocean felt close, maintaining a steady drum beat above the insect hum. The evening felt poised on the edge of a great stillness. He breathed in and out again and again, letting go of murderous behemoths, belligerent tradies and drought flattened earth. The Milky Way kept drawing his attention upwards and away. He smoked a joint and gaped up mesmerized. The lone camper felt the weed soften and refine his awareness. The solitude felt like luxury. It was so good to be finally alone and on holiday from a dry riven world. He poured himself another glass and sat back in stoned satisfaction at the prospect of doing nothing till bedtime. A moment later he heard a car engine revving in the distance. Then headlights appeared, a blazing battery of them on blinding high beam. They roamed and lurched about like some drunken thing gunning down the little tracks of the park.

The lone camper felt a tremor of panic run up his spine. The driver was erratic, slowing and speeding at intervals, hopping about like some hurt animal in pursuit of prey. The national park camp ground was big but the camper could see the jumping lights getting closer. They jagged and bounced across the low scrub and into the encircling banksia shooting for shadows. The lone camper flinched. The lights turned a corner and came straight towards him on retina busting high beam. The driver gunned his engine again and picked up speed. Despite everything the lone camper decided to stay seated. He was glad he was stoned and took another long sip of wine. The car raced down the sandy track before breaking violently. It swung past his camp site, did a quick arc and jolted to a sudden stop, lights still on high, with loud twangy country music blaring.

The lone camper remained seated and shut his eyes against the interrogating light. He lowered his head a little and cradled the glass of wine in his hands. His thoughts were racing. The intrusion spelt danger. Maybe it was hoons or local boys looking for excitement.

He was not so far off the beaten track but he had heard stories. He was stoned and on his own. He had only enough self-defense skill to get himself into trouble. He took another sip of wine and decided sitting still was the better part of valour. He looked away from the blinding lights and waited.

The country music kept up its strident twang. The lone camper felt some relief. Hoons were likely to be playing head banging music. He watched the car door open and a man lurch out holding a stubby. He staggered and swayed unsteadily holding his stubby high in the air and then reached back in to the car to kill the engine and the lights with the music still whining. He took a big swig from his stubby and came lurching towards the fire.

"Ya not one of those greeny lefty leso lovin poofters are ya? If ya are, I'm gunna have to shoot ya!"

The man swung his free arm extravagantly in the air and nearly stumbled. As he came into the fire light the lone camper could see he was a thick set overweight man anywhere from his mid-sixties to his seventies. He belched loudly and swung his head back to get better look at the lone camper. He was wearing a tattered red flannelette shirt and smelt of spilt beer and anger. Even in the fire light his eyes looked blood shot and his face bristled with a ten day old beard. He took another extravagant swig and swayed closer.

"So, what are ya then?" the drunk stranger burped his question. "Ya look sus to me. Only good greeny is a dead greeny." He swayed back and looked momentarily satisfied with the world. "Maybe ya one of those useless labour pricks that shit all over us with red tape. Tree hugging Canberra poofters! Always wingeing about those bastards on welfare. We should shoot the lot of em! Or that Bob Brown prick! What a stuck up arsehole! Him and his leso, homo mates. We should've dropped him off a cliff long ago. Ya not a greeny are ya?" the drunk asked again, clearly not convinced.

The lone camper could see the dangerous light in the drunk's eyes. He stood up and smiled. "Nah! Mate" he lied easily, putting on his best flat Aussie accent. "'Too much trouble for me" He added, knowing it wasn't that far from the truth. "Have a seat." He indicated a sawn-off log a previous camper had left at his camp site.

"Too fuckin right! The stranger belched again before sitting down abruptly. "Can't have any more greenies out here! Bastards! Be good if we can shoot the whole fuckin lot of em! I fought and bled for this country and look what they do. Bastards don't know shit. So up themselves. Think they can look down their snooty noses at those of us who fought. Think we can live on daises and sunshine like all those stupid hippies back in the old days. They don't know shit!"

"Who does?" the lone camper responded mildly.

"Not those useless pricks in Canberra. Don't know their arse from their mouths. And all their tree hugging poofter mates. All they want to do is fuck over real working people and bury everyone in shit loads of red tape. Think this big world owes 'em a livin! It fuckin doesn't! Fuckin arsonists! Not one of those lazy green shit heads have seen a war. Not one of 'em has a clue what to do when the world turns to shit!" The stranger took another long swig from his stubby and glared hard at the lone camper. His eye brows were flared in suspicion as he searched the lone camper's face for a reaction. The camper just nodded and waited for the man to go on. It was easy to believe the angry stranger had a gun and didn't need much excuse to use it.

"You ever been in a war?" The stranger half snapped half slurred his question.

"None of the hot ones" the lone camper said mildly and regretted being too clever. The stranger belched again and glared harder. "What the fuck is that supposed to mean?"

"Just being alive and getting by."

"Fuck that!" the stranger spat. "I was in Vietnam. Saw stuff that would make your girly boy balls fall off. Dead set! Unless one of the gooks made you eat them or shove em up ya own arse. War! You never get used to it! Boys like you have spent all your life on cut lawns. Ya know nothing about how raw and shit blown it can get. Nothin!"

"I agree." The lone camper was in no mood for an argument. "I was too young for Vietnam. Then Gough came in and turned it all upside down."

"Another treacherous cunt!" the veteran spat again. "Told a whole lotta lily livered boys like you that the world owes ya a living. It fuckin doesn't! Not one bit! Everything is tooth and nail. Everything only comes hard! Life is just a shit show. Then you are dead! Life is a real bitch! A real hard bitch that will fuck you sideways as soon as look at ya."

"Gee." The lone camper still managed to sound mild. He wondered if he should offer the veteran a joint but quickly thought better of it. "It must have been really difficult," he offered diffidently.

The veterans face softened into a sad scowl whilst he rubbed his free hand through his short wiry hair. "You don't know the half of it. Never! I fuckin try to forget. It was a fuckin shit hole of a country. Gave me all kinds of skin problems and now I wake up freezing even though the place was always hotter than hell."

The lone camper said nothing.

The veteran glared and belched and took another long swig and then tossed his bottle at the fire. It bounced and rolled under the lone camper's feet. Nearby the country music still whined. The veteran stood up as abruptly as he sat down.

"Are you okay?'" the lone camper asked carefully.

The veteran swaggered back to his jeep and jarred the door open.

"Nah mate, still deciding whether I should shoot ya or not. Nah I'm not okay. But no quick exit for me. Not me mate! Nah, from now on its just one big slow kick in the head. Enjoy ya fire. Next time it won't be so pretty." He got in slammed the door and jerked the jeep violently into motion. The lone camper watched the jeep blunder erratically out of sight.

Only slowly did the night grow still again. The lone camper felt a tight hard ache in his chest like some kind of fear and trauma. No longer did he feel free and alone. The quarrelling possums had already decided to go back into the safety of the dark.

He picked up the drunk stranger's bottle and emptied his own glass. He stared long and hard at the fire.

His chest still kept hurting. It was as if some raging, ripping, snarling thing was trying to beat its way out.

He wasn't sure who it belonged to.

26

The Militant Devotees

It had the elements of a bad joke. A Zen monk, an organic farmer from Wales and a garden variety diocesan seminarian were in a vegetarian restaurant in South India discussing enlightenment. They all agreed, none of them knew what it was.

The Zen monk thought that whatever it was, it was wasted on the young. He was Californian cool with his hip Ray Ban sunglasses, grey robes, crew cut and long plaited ponytail. He was older than the other men but seemed younger. He ate slowly, taking his time to make more become even more. He was telling the others that ashram life was a piece a cake. He seemed very amused. They didn't agree.

The muggy tropical afternoon was wearing on and they were eating as much they wanted. The fast-talking Welsh farmer was over ashrams. He was sharing a room with a crazed follower of Sai Baba who was fasting himself to death. The five o'clock starts and meagre vegetarian food did nothing for the soul he said and even less for the body. What India lacked was entrepreneurial initiative. There was too much fatalism. Back home on his farm they were green engineering for a new future as the climate changed. He kept talking as fast as he ate. He was a techno optimist and an unapologetic pagan. The spirit was everywhere he said. You didn't need to go to an ashram to see it. Back home he had seen spirits, auras and fairies in the Welsh hills. A new dynamic age of the spirit was already there for those daring enough to take it. The old religions needed to get out of the way.

The Australian seminarian had gone a bit feral. India was wearing him down. He was more bemused than amused. Somewhere along the way his old religion had gone missing. The exclusive Christ had taken up yoga and turned churches into temples. The Alpha and Omega had segued to a total "*Om.*" What was exclusive now was shockingly cosmic and inclusive. His church and God had proven too small. He was in too much confusion to talk so he mostly nodded and listened.

The cool Zen monk told them his monastery would break them both within a week no matter how fit they were. That was more or less the idea. Only the broken were enlightened. Everyone else was fooling themselves but they were likely too young yet to understand.

The Welshman asked if Zen monks were celibate. The Zen monk just laughed and asked if he used magic mushrooms to see his fairies. The Welshman got a bit testy and asked what was wrong with that. The monk just laughed and said his monastery was co-sexual but no one took any vow to be celibate. They were just too tired and exhausted from staring at white walls to be bothered. The seminarian just kept his head down.

The food kept coming. The Zen monk told them that this was as good as it gets and not to worry about being enlightened. He could vouch for it personally that the quest for enlightenment was one insult after another. The more you grasped, the less you got. As it turned out, staring down white walls had been quite informative.

The other men were inclined to agree. Enlightenment might not be what it was cracked up to be. They both had ashram hangovers and were inclined to outsource asceticism to the future. Rather than get the bus back they decided to take a tourist walk and check out the local temples.

The outside heat weighed them down as much as their full bellies. They ambled through the afternoon heat marvelling at one of the multi-storey, many coloured temples. The busy street rolled on past them. The temple had a whole pantheon of gods protecting it secrets. The gods rose above them in a gaudy riot of legs and arms and painted eyes, defying sobriety and modesty. If they were idols, none of them cared to apologise for it.

When the tourists got to the temple entrance they discovered they were not allowed in. The Zen monk just looked bemused at being characterised as an unbeliever. The Welshman looked offended. The seminarian was relieved. His new Christ might be bigger than his old one but he was not sure if he would be welcome amongst so many alien Gods. He soon got an answer.

The first they heard of it was the chanting. Not the mumbling drone of heat struck Brahmins or temple devotees but the sound and tramp of an approaching host. They heard them for quite some time before they saw them. They were all men's voices; loud, militant and angry. They sounded like an advancing army or an angry lynch mob. Suddenly the busy street ran for cover. Even the cool Californian no longer looked amused. There was an edge in the air that had not been there before. The locals had gone to ground.

The chanting grew more raucous. Moments later the tourists saw a baying army round the corner. Discreetly the three of them moved well to the side of the road. There were hundreds and hundreds of men all clad in black shawls and dhotis. The Zen monk looked curious; the Welsh farmer looked anxious and the seminarian quietly reached for his Jesus beads.

The army marched on under the banner of a large black swastika. There was no saffron to be seen. Everything about them shouted rage. The seminarian told them that the swastika was in fact an ancient Hindu symbol appropriated by the Nazis. The Zen monk joked and said it looked like the Hindus wanted it back real bad. The Welshman told them he was terrified. He had seen too many swastikas at the movies. A fascist was fascist be they Indian or anybody. Who else would march under such a symbol?

The Welshman and the seminarian could feel fear tingling and rising up from the soles of their feet. They huddled further to the side but the Zen monk just stared and smiled as the chanters got close. It looked like a tide of black was covering the street defying all colour. Not even the gaudy pantheon seemed a match for the rising dark. The Welshman suggested they should disappear but the Zen monk had other ideas.

Out of the blue the Zen monk quietly asked out loud; "I really wonder what these dudes are tripping about. Man, are they intense!"

The seminarian sucked in his breath. The Welshman was furious with the Zen monk who seemingly even found a lynch mob amusing. Neither of them got a word out before a neat bespectacled intelligent looking young man separated out of the marchers and came towards them. He was accompanied by a small circle of fellow black-robed devotees. He said: "I would like to tell you what we are about."

The three tourists just stared at each other. The exact mirroring of the Zen monk's question was not lost on any of them. The edge in the air felt dangerous and sharp. The intelligent young man's face was awash with earnest conviction. He wagged his head and smiled.

"We are all here on Lord Shiva's command." The young man smiled and spoke good English but his voice was tight with hostility.

"Yes, yes, yes," his fellow devotees chirped in. "Yes, yes, we all saw Lord Shiva's lightning!" They all wagged their heads in unison. "We all saw! Over two hundred thousand of us all saw the sign." They nodded grimly together.

The bespectacled young man went on. "Yes, we are returning from the shrine. We all saw the bolt of lightning straight out of a blue sky. No clouds!"

"Yes, yes, " the others chirped. "We all saw!"

"That many of you saw it?" the Zen monk did not sound convinced.

"Yes, yes, maybe even more!" the young man wagged his head and smiled fiercely.

"Why the sign?" the Zen monk appeared fascinated.

"It is simple," the young man wagged his head with the others. "We all saw his anger and his fire."

"It's simple?"

"Yes, Lord Shiva has commanded that we drive all the Muslims and all the Christians out of India. They are invaders and polluters. They have done great harm to our land. Great harm! We will not rest until they are either all driven out or destroyed."

There was an uneasy pause. The tourists exchanged glances. The seminarian was glad the Zen monk looked neither Christian nor Muslim. He was glad he himself had gone feral. The Welshman just leaned across and whispered very quietly in his ear.

"Is this some kind of bad joke? If you want to be a martyr and tell them you are a Christian, I will kill you first."

The Zen monk just looked on and smiled. He seemed more amused than ever. His companions were annoyed. It seemed the black army was giving the Buddhists a leave pass. They were relieved to see the bespectacled young man and his companions take up their war chant and move on.

After that none of them wanted to do any more sightseeing. Ashram life suddenly seemed appealing even if they didn't know what enlightenment was. As soon as the street was clear they made their way back to the bus.

The seminarian's mind was a whirl. Shiva's soldier had told them quite a story. He did not want to be a martyr. Lord Shiva sounded like a god not to be trifled with. He wasn't sure if Christ was big enough for India or Lord Shiva.

It was time to roll out the yoga mat and find out.

27

The Armchair Revolutionary

"Well fuck me sideways! Will you bloody look at that!"

The armchair revolutionary was fulminating at a safe distance. "Just bloody look!" He raised his right arm to the flat thin air. "This is how our world is ending!" He raved on in a reasonable facsimile of outrage whilst he struggled to find the mute button for the remote control. "Yes!" he raised his voice over the clamour of advertising for another reality show. There were cheesy no name celebrities surviving weekend warrior boot camp and playing combat golf in swimming pools. They had the temerity to interrupt the cricket. "Yes!" he fumed on "Not with a bang but an endless fucking whimper."

He looked away as one of the celebrities dangled from a high tower, turning vertiginous terror into viewing pleasure. As usual no one answered back, especially dead poets. A moment later, when the cricket resumed, his tight cameo of outrage was over. He liked watching the grass grow. He liked the subversive lack of haste in the battle between ball and bat. Cricket was the sound and essence of summer languor. It gave him every excuse to remain in his chair until the next set of commercials set him off again.

"Look, look!" he started fuming again, not quite prepared to admit that the advertisements were where all the action was. This time another group of nameless celebrities were swapping partners quicker than they could change underwear.

The space between overs gave him all the time he needed to make his views clear. Rage could be rationed if you had a mind for it. The culture was banal. The culture was sick. The culture was morally bankrupt. The armchair revolutionary was good at observing the metrics of decline. He was good at espousing just causes. He knew that the empire was in trouble and that the emperor had no clothes. He could tell you in tight dot points how it was all going to hell in a hand basket. He could give facts and figures about the slow burn of late capitalism. How the rich were getting obscenely richer and the poor ever poorer. He could tell you the world was burning; habitats were being lost, wild places were fast disappearing, Forests were decimated, oceans were turning acid, plastic was choking life, tipping points had arrived and they were over the cliff and falling. He could tell you that the media, corporate power, the government and even the churches were all in on preserving the status quo. They all had a hand in the tyranny and distracting everyone with bread and circuses. He knew it. Even sitting in his armchair he could feel the cruelty and exploitation coming home to roost. The centre would not hold. Whatever thin patina of morality the culture offered would not be enough to hold it. A chasm was widening between the oppressed and the oppressors, the times were tinder dry for conflagration. Revolution was coming if only he could get out of his armchair.

Watching the grass grow was easier. So long as there was cricket, the revolution could wait. He sank back in his chair too numbed to feel the burn of real despair and too distracted to notice that the cricket was his reality television of choice. Getting vexed between overs was all the rage he was prepared to spend. Getting involved was too painful. It was summer holiday time after all, and if rough beasts were slouching towards Jerusalem, he was in no mood to argue with them.

In the next gap between overs there was a news broadcast that nearly had him standing. Strange and amazing things were happening to the empire across the oceans. The news was sensational. The citadel of empire had been breached. Angry thugs wrapped in flags and carrying lynch ropes along with kooky gun lovers and bellicose bible bangers had seized the capital. They were marching in enraged solidarity spurred on by their celebrity emperor. The revolution was at hand and it was not what he was expecting. Instead of ending the oppression the slaves were agitating for more slavery.

The armchair revolutionary shook his head. How could such a grotesque demagogue garner so much support? How come they could not see how murderous and mendacious the celebrity fascist really was? Didn't they know whose side they were on?

As usual there was other news. There was the weather, the stock market, and all the business-as-usual rolling along as it usually did. And then there was something about some sort of virus in China. A few pointy heads were frowning and telling people to get worried. He flicked to another channel and another set of celebrities offering themselves for ritual humiliation.

Eventually he flicked back to the cricket. This time he kept the mute on between overs. He needed comfort in order to maintain his rage. His chair was just the place. But with the sound on mute he almost imagined he could hear another dead poet whispering outrages in the ether. It was a subversive anthem he once believed in:

'Do not go gently....rage, rage against the dying of the light.'

There had been a time when those words burned. Once upon a time he had been ready to strike the necessary blows. Back then his bones were packed with certainty. Black was black and white was white. But somewhere along the line the world had shape shifted under a thousand shades of grey. Somewhere his heart had grown tepid and his body old and fat. It had been much easier to criticise than to get involved. Now he also was just another slave.

The armchair revolutionary shifted uneasily in his seat. Another voice whispered subversively in the muted air.

"Feed my sheep, feed my sheep, feed my lambs."

He lost all interest in the cricket. His analysis was as cheap as chips. Who summoned him so unceremoniously? Someone demanding more honesty and courage than he had. Someone ready to refuse the luxury of despair. Someone who did not allow distractions to displace reality. Someone who never thought love was a lost cause. Someone who would not allow stupidity and vacuity be turned into virtue. Yes! There had been a time when that voice had also whispered 'rage, rage, against the dying of the light.'

It was no armchair revolutionary who had commanded him to take the log out of his own eye and leave splinters for better doctors. No cheesy celebrity who ever craved attention was so imperative. No politician reducing the common good to a blood sport had ever spoken thus. Who else had so deliberately walked right into the belly of the beast?

The armchair revolutionary shook his head again. The cricket was suddenly boring. There were voices in his head he could not ignore. Whose side was he on? The revolution was always at hand. One where the poor, the naked, the disposed and oppressed were first and all the naked emperors last. There was a revolutionary who had scattered the proud in their conceit and sent the rich away empty. One who faced down the heart of darkness with the heart mercy. He had lit a fire none of the naked emperors could ever put out.

The armchair revolutionary sighed sadly. It had been a long time since that fire had shifted his feet and warmed his bones. For too long he had sat in his chair inside a prison without walls.

The summons still remained.

'Feed my sheep'

Suddenly the cricket blared into his awareness.

"Bowled him!"

The commentators were abuzz with excitement.

The armchair revolutionary got up, turned off the television and walked.

28

The Auschwitz Survivor

"You have no idea how a man will dance when a gun is firing at his feet." The old Auschwitz survivor chuckled but his eyes were misty. "The Americans were very angry at what they saw. They left us the guns. We waited a long time to see that dance." He chuckled again, choosing his words slowly. "Their commanding officer tried to put a stop to it but his men left the guns in front of the gate." He chuckled again. "Yes, nothing like a machine gun to get a man dancing. The Americans didn't think justice should wait and neither did we." The old Auschwitz survivor's face crinkled into a merry smile.

"Was that at Auschwitz?" the visitor from the lucky country could only gape in utter incomprehension. The Auschwitz survivor was telling him stories no one would believe. There were photographs spread out in his lap of gaunt men in striped pyjamas carrying huge lumps of stone up a hill. They were like Sisyphus, condemned to unremitting torment, sentenced to hellish labour from which death was the only escape. On top of all the photographs was the one

showing the entrance to the camp. There it was, written in hard rusted iron, spelling the cruel lie conceived in the heart of darkness:
Arbreit Macht Frei --- Work makes you free

The lucky visitor was trying to not let his jaw drop to the floor. What a stupendously cynical lie. Even more than half a century later and on the underside of the world, the sheer effrontery and audacity of it left him breathless. How effortlessly propaganda justified evil. How many souls had looked up at that grim lie, not prepared for the outrage and suffering that awaited? He knew that he, for one, would have no idea whatsoever.

"No," the old Pole hadn't stopped chuckling. "They took us Poles as slave labour. When the Russians got near they took us further west. They thought the Americans would be kinder." He chuckled again.

The Auschwitz survivor was on a roll. He wasn't used to being listened to. His lucky visitor could only nod in sympathy. The visitor was born in a soft, far-away land, accustomed to outsourcing war for off-shore purposes. He found himself hearing about things he could not imagine. No wonder the old man's wife didn't want to listen nor his surly and sullen adult children. The visitor had sympathy for them too. He had not been born under such a shadow. His own birth did not seem such a precarious occasion. He had not inherited such a well-spring of sadness that, no matter how much you resisted, always ended up sinking into your bones by peculiar osmosis. He had not felt the same proximity to oblivion. Perhaps if he had, he might have bet everything on denial. He also would have disdained everything but the pragmatic present. Just like the old man's children resenting their fate, he too would have had no time for the old survivor's God and his memorabilia.

The listening was not easy. The old man giggled quite a lot and took the long way around each story. He told the soft-lander how he had joined the resistance after the Nazis razed his homeland. The

Gestapo had arrested him and had him tortured. The main reason he survived was that he was very young, and Polish and not a Jew. He was lucky enough to be part of the slave labour the Nazis used to run the camp. They gave him clerical duties which, along with being young and strong was what kept him alive .Strangely his face shone as he talked.

"How old were you?" the lucky visitor was still trying not to gape.

"Fifteen," the old man looked steadily at him, his face proud and defiant.

"Fifteen!" the visitor was incredulous.

"Yes!" the old man nodded emphatically, still the proud nationalist. "I was a small fish. We only ever had five names they could get out of us." He sighed and went very quiet.

"But they broke you?" the visitor could hardly believe what he was asking.

The old man's face still shone despite the sorrow in his eyes. "Yes, they interviewed my mother." He chuckled again and gave the visitor a wry nod.

"God!" the visitor tried not to gasp. There was a long silence before the old man spoke again.

"Well," he let the word hang in the air for a long time. "What can you do?"

The soft visitor knew he had absolutely no idea. The old man started to talk about how they used to take it turns to sleep inside his crowded hut just as his wife came into the room with tea and biscuits. As she bustled and fussed, Auschwitz and its horrors seem to disappear. She chatted breezily about her dog and the weather and baking and the garden. There was no mention of war. The visitor could see the steel in her sad eyes and could only wonder how hard it must have been trying to forget so much unholy outrage.

When she left, the war came back into the room. There was a question the visitor had to ask.

"But you have only just returned from Auschwitz after more than fifty years. Why ever would you go back?"

The old man tried to fight down a coughing spasm. The double pneumonia he had caught on the way back had nearly killed him. It was a long time before he spoke.

"Well," he smiled a long, sad smile. "I was in love." His chuckle was brief. He reached across and showed the visitor a photo of a very elderly lady with very sad eyes standing on some unknown street. The Auschwitz survivor watched him intently.

"The Dutch film crew found me after all this time. She was younger than me. A Jew. Very pretty. They gave her clerical duties like me. We used to hold hands when no one was looking. We told each other how much we were in love. When they marched us away I thought I would never see her again. I thought she was dead." The old man's face clouded with pain. "And then the Dutch wanted us to get together in Auschwitz. They wanted to do a documentary."

"And your wife went back with you?"

"Yes," the old man's attempt to laugh ended in another coughing spasm. "She wasn't very pleased." There was another silence.

"Did they meet?"

"Of course. She is very old now like me. She was married but is a widow now."

The old man said nothing more. The visitor's head was still full of questions. What was it like to reach across the chasm of time and chance? Was he still in love? Did it break his heart again? How hard was it for his wife? But the day was wearing and the old man was looking frail. It was clear enough the return trip taken a mortal toll. They spoke a bit more about the documentary and about Europe before the visitor made to leave. He shifted in his chair but the old survivor gestured for him to stay.

"I brought you this." He reached across his desk and unwrapped a picture covered in brown paper. "Our lady of Czestochowa," he said, proudly.

The lucky visitor took the image reverently in his hands and stared at the black Madonna.

'How strange,' he thought. It struck him then that a black Madonna was a fitting divine icon for someone surviving such a holocaust. Her deep earthy serenity and ample maternity might say more than a tortured broken body strung up on an instrument of death. Somehow there was something more bearable about a loving maternal gaze not looking away from the evil of the world than a naked dying man on a cross. The mute Madonna was inscrutable. She stared back at him with a stern calm. Her dark face seemed able to countenance it all. Her wounded beauty told the visitor one thing. The old man was still in love. Whether it was with God or the girl from Auschwitz he did not know. The past and the present felt like they were touching held together by a woman's gaze.

The old man had the double pneumonia to prove it.

"How are you now?" the visitor asked the Auschwitz's survivor, unsure if he was ready for his answer.

The old man just chuckled

"God is God," he said. "I am ready."

29

The Mzungu

"*Mzungu! Mzungu*"

The little ones waited most of the morning. The man from distant worlds was coming. When the battered four-wheel drive appeared, they began cheering and singing. They ran down the goat track in a chanting throng of colour. Most of them had never seen a white man before. As soon as the man from the sky stepped out, they were all over him.

"*Mzungu! Mzungu!*" they cheered and sang almost toppling him over. Behind the little ones, older children were singing doing a simple two step easy rhythm.

"We are very happy to see you. You are very welcome here."

The man who had flown over oceans and deserts and war zones stepped forward. Already some of the little ones were trying to swing from his beard whilst others curiously pinched the blond hair on his arms. Everywhere there was clapping and drumming and singing and wide smiles and flashing white teeth. Everyone was chanting;

"*Mzungu! Mzungu!*"

Little hands were all over him, reaching for his own like a human river sweeping him along. No one in the little village really knew his name. No one knew where he lived. No one knew how cold and distant it was. No one knew how different. All they knew was that the man from the sky was a *mzungu* priest and that every *mzungu* was rich beyond imagination.

The *mzungu* wiped his brow and tried to match the smiles. He was pole-axed by the humidity and had a splitting insomnia headache. The jet lag had faded but not the culture shock. It had been a long drive from the compound, guarded by men with machine guns. His back hurt from the ride over broken roads, past fields of withered maize and stunted coffee. Everywhere there were signs of drought and want and raw poverty. The local priest was a farmer's son. He told the *mzungu* they had no doubt the climate was changing. Even if his people did not know about *mzungus* they were on intimate terms with global warming.

The *mzungu* laughed and held up his hands in surrender and let the river take him. The little ones ushered him towards the simple tumbled-down brick hut they called a school. The sight, combined with their eager welcome wrenched his heart. There were no windows or chairs or desks save for what the teacher used. There was just a broken concrete floor to sit on. Only the blackboard on the wall along with a few pieces of broken chalk showed the purpose of the building. The *mzungu* swayed and smiled while the children continued their two-step. It was a long while before all the drumming and singing came to an end.

Then the local priest, acting as a translator asked the *mzungu* to say something. The school was cramped and the air was close. He had no idea of what to say. He let go of one of the little ones hands, took up a piece of chalk and walked over to the blackboard and drew a map. He stepped back and waved the chalk like a wand hoping it might improve his cartography.

I am from Australia," he said still smiling. "Does anyone know where that is?" The local priest translated as he spoke.

The *mzungu* stepped back to look at his map. He had seen grade two children draw better. No one in the stuffy room said a word. The *mzungu* pressed on feeling like a fraud.

"It is over here," he said as he drew a big wide circle that was supposed to be the planet. The local priest kept translating while the *mzungus* map got tangled up in squiggles and bent lines.

The *mzungu* stepped back to survey his work. The local priest had stopped translating. No one else spoke or put their hands up.

The *mzungu* kept on bravely smiling.

''Australia is on the other side of the world across the ocean and faraway."

Everyone kept looking at him expectantly. They were waiting for him to say something they could understand. The *mzungu* stole another look at his preschool standard map and frowned. It struck him that he might as well be talking about one of the far moons of Saturn. As far as they were concerned, he had fallen out of the sky from a spaceship arriving from out of the back end of the solar system.

How could he tell them he was from another time and place? His people no longer believed in the old dispensation. They were busy clutching other gods now. They were cross pressured, worried and self-entitled. Two thousand years of familiarity had bred two thousand years' worth of contempt. Faith was not so simple or vigorous back on his far away moon. Back in that alien land his people went shopping instead of going to church. Back there, they were bruised and beaten down by scandal. Back on his flashy moon filled with shining machines the little school house in Africa might as well have been in another universe.

The *mzungu* kept smiling to keep up his courage. Looking outside he saw signs of the lack of rain everywhere he looked. He could feel the aura of hunger in the air. Every face held his own keenly. He was the only fat person in the room. He sucked in his gut feeling guilty and ashamed and went on. Every face remained expectant. They knew he was rich. He had power. He was a sign of solidarity. He was a *mzungu* after all.

The *mzungu* kept talking and praised them all for their robust and dynamic faith. He did not tell them how he had all but lost his own. He told them that they were all missionaries now. That he had come to show them they were not on their own. Back on his moon, they were all held in prayer and support. He did not tell them they all had more resilience in each little finger than a fat man like him had in all his bones.

Luckily for the *mzungu* the teacher broke in and started talking over him. There was some giggles and shy smiles. Some girls came forward and started their own two-step dance. The rest of the school clapped and sang. The *mzungu* also clapped and swayed and two-stepped, showing them all how white men cannot dance. Just when he thought he was off the hook the local priest asked him for a word of faith.

The *mzungu* fought down his panic. He started talking about the miracle of the loaves and fishes. He did not tell them he no longer believed in miracles like they all did. He told them that they were all part of one family both the living and the dead and that each one had a gift to give. They all nodded. They all knew what it was like to talk to the dead. Back on his moon the dead were quickly forgotten.

The *mzungu* kept talking. He told them they were all held by God's love. He neglected to say he barely believed such a thing. He did not tell them they should always look for the details in the fine print. Instead of telling them God was a consuming fire he told them God was living bread. The air was dense and hot. The crops outside were sagging with fatigue. The *mzungu* could see they had seen fire enough. He was the one with fat to burn. So, he kept on talking and waffling and waving his hands in circles about God and family and love until some boys and girls got up for another two-step. Everyone clapped and sang and swayed and once more little hands and fingers started pinching and pulling.

The *mzungu* swayed and clapped too. No one had a clue what he said. It did not matter. All they had to do was touch him and be with him. Anything was possible after that! *Mzungus* came from glittering worlds. They had power, they had resources, and they had money. They never suffered want or hunger. *Mzungus* made the world go round.

The two-step dancers upped the tempo. Soon they were all pulling him back outside. The *mzungu* let little hands pull and guide. He was a rock star! He was a celebrity! He was a walking, talking, living answer to their prayers. He swayed along beginning to feel much more pleased with himself until on the way out a mother blocked his path and thrust her baby into his arms for a blessing. Everyone was smiling and clapping. The *mzungu* was smiling and clapping too.

But not the baby.

As soon as the baby got a close look at his *mzungu* face, the infant screamed in terror. His blessing become an exorcism. The *mzungu* tried not to flinch. The baby was in no doubt about who had the demon. Lucky for him the clapping and dancing kept going. Only the baby was the wiser. Everyone else just kept on smiling.

The human river moved the *mzungu* on and then formed a circle. One of the men stepped forward and thrust a spade into his hands. There was a tree to be planted in his honour. The *mzungu* took the spade and started digging until they laughed and pushed him aside. Clearly, he was no farmer. So, they dug and planted and manured and mulched while he looked on. He did not tell them he thought he might have wasted his life; that it might have been better if he were a simple gardener rather than a manager of sanctuaries the *mzungus* no longer cared for. Instead he blessed the tree and said a prayer of thanks. All the while the boys and girls kept singing;

"We are very happy to see you. You are very welcome here."

Days later, the man from the skies returned over deserts and seas and war zones. He stopped over in Dubai with time to kill. While he waited, he did laps of the terminal. No one was laughing or clapping or dancing. The only smiles on offer looked like smiles for hire. Now the *mzungu* was pulled along by another river. This time no little hands tugged in welcome. He could smell the reek of slavery in the air. It was lying just out of reach behind air brushed pieties and advertising displays. He could smell the hypocrisy. No matter which religion was on top, all the feasting was at mammon's banquet.

A few hours later the *mzungu's* spaceship took to the air. It did a lap of the slave owner's high towers and went south to his distant moon. He was glad to be gone. He sighed and drew in his breath. It was a long flight and his head was full of questions. Who was he, if not a gardener or a priest? Was he just another mammon loving hypocrite? A failed sanctuary manager? A white man too stiff for dancing? Was he nothing but left-over dust in the air, nothing more than a twig floating or sinking on cruel seas? Was he just a fat middleman blocking the door? A sideshow spruiker for second hand gods? Did he have any faith at all?

The *mzungu* was too tired for answers. He closed his eyes and saw the children dancing and clapping in welcome. Behind them there was a tree with his name on it.

Somewhere in Africa an orange tree was transfigured in evening light.

30

The Scruffy Bodhisattva

Christmas day in Hazaribagh was another working day. It was warm and the tourist had washing to do. He was far from home and relishing the fact that not everyone in the world celebrated Christmas. There was no tinsel; no jingle bell muzak, no monetized mirth; no Santa slaves in red hats; no schlocky carols, no glittering plastic pine trees in corporate foyers and not a single fat man in a red suit anywhere to be seen.

The streets were busy. Trucks and moto taxis played chicken with each another, horns blaring defiantly. Pedestrians and cows mingled in the streets. Men on overladen bicycles and women in bright saris with heavy loads on their heads jostled each other calmly. He had been up since dawn. The breakfast of chapattis and vegetables would have been a thin feast back home. It was all they had to offer before another hard day in the fields. He still felt hungry but he was content. The night before was where the action was. He had seen the manger. He had gone back in time. The goats and the chickens and the children all did dances. They sung *bhajans* for hours. They lifted up the cup and broke the bread. They ran amok around the village, banging drums and telling any Muslim or Hindu who cared that God had pitched his tent amongst them. They even asked the tourist for a song but begged him to stop when he started singing the Lord's Prayer. He did not mind. He was content. He could swap pilgrimaging for touring now. In only two days' time he would be on the other side of India sunning himself on the beach in Goa. The Christ child had been born again. From now on Christ would have his work cut out making all things new. The tourist thought it better to leave it to him and the Jesuits. Goa and holidays beckoned.

By the time he got back to the retreat house he was back in his own time. Everything was quiet. The Jesuits had gone to ground in all the excitement. Only the cawing crows and vultures riding thermals paid any attention. It was as good a time as any to wash clothes and poach some pegs from the line. The tourist did not see the stranger approach.

"How long are you in for?"

"Eh?"

The tourist spun around sharply. He saw a man in a torn orange T-shirt standing there with a wide gap-toothed smile. He was middle aged with a sagging gut and bald head. He looked tattered and dishevelled and quite pleased with himself. He smiled a broad and mischievous smile and asked again:

"How long are you in for?"

"What?" the tourist looked up at the swirling vultures none the wiser. Close by the crows were gossiping and arguing loudly. The scruffy gap-toothed man just laughed out loud.

"Here," the stranger spoke with an educated, upper-class accent that the tourist couldn't put his finger on. He sounded a bit Indian or a bit British and somehow also Australian. He might have been mid-Atlantic or mid- Pacific by the timbre of his voice. He sounded quite amused as he spoke. "Here in *Bharat*."

"What and where is *Bharat*?" the tourist was confused.

"Here! You have that look that I only ever see here. You have that look. Half lost, half found and a bit too dazed to know the difference." The gap-toothed stranger's smile got larger. "Here in India! The jewel in the crown, the most ancient of nations, the land of saints, sinners and beggars. Here! The kindest and the cruellest country in the world."

"Oh," the tourist nodded, trying not to look slow headed as he caught the scruffy man's meaning. "I have been here just a few weeks."

"Not long enough."

"Long enough for me!"

The stranger laughed. "No, you are still only half found and half lost. India has a lot more work to do with you yet. You need a few more seasons or a few more life times."

"What for?" the tourist just wanted to get on with his holiday.

"To find out who you are and what you want to be."

"I already know that." The tourist was not in a mood to be patronized.

"Do you? Really?" the scruffy man had a gleam in his eye. "Are you a saint or a sinner or a beggar? They're all popular here."

"I'm just a tourist."

"How disappointing. I was hoping you might be a *bodhisattva* in hiding. You might find one of them anywhere in our cruel imperilled world but they are particularly fond of India." The stranger winked and then grew serious. "But time is on your side. There is time enough to fall over yet. I have. You should try it. You might progress to a homeless nomad or even a poor pilgrim. Sooner than you think you will be a beggar or a saint or both. So where are you going, Mr Tourist?" The scruffy man beamed widely again.

"Goa." The tourist suddenly felt a bit sheepish about his destination. "I have had enough of ordeal soaked out-back India. I need a beach to lie on."

"Goa." The gap-toothed man whistled through his teeth theatrically. He gave the tourist a searching look.

"Plenty of better beaches back home don't you think? Plenty of ordeals of one sort or another walking the streets of Goa right now. You have that classic first world blind spot. Why not go east to Calcutta and do something original with your life?" the gap-toothed man broke out into another chuckle.

The tourist was aghast. He became intemperate. "Shit! How long exactly have you been in 'here?'" he waved irritably at the vultures. "I've seen enough of the pain, the crowds, and the poverty thank you very much. Why would anyone want to go to Calcutta?"

"To suffer and get a spiritual education," the stranger laughed. "Maybe because what you are called to do is more important than what you want to do. Maybe because the way to enlightenment is one ordeal after another. That is what any teacher worth their salt will tell you. It is one insult after another all the way down, believe me." The gap-toothed man was still grinning.

"God! Just how long have you been here?" the tourist gave the vultures another wave.

"Ever since I hit rock bottom. I had a long way to fall. Lots of insults." A shadow of sadness shifted the grin from the strangers face. "You might say I was compelled to fall apart. Like most of us I handled all my hurt the wrong way. Subsequently I lost it all. Why else would I come here?"

"For a holiday?" The tourist did not like what he was hearing.

"Oh, every day is a holiday now. Everything is a gift," the scruffy man flashed the tourist a damaged smile. "Lessons you learn from the bottom."

"There has to be an easier way," the tourist protested.

"The easy way is never easy." The stranger kept grinning. "That is one thing I learnt at the house of the dying. That; and how to survive food riots during the pre-monsoon build up. It has taken me quite a while to put the weight back on." The stranger patted his gut affectionately.

"Shit! You went to the house of the dying for a holiday!" The tourist was having trouble being temperate. "Why would you do that?"

"The Dalai Lama sent me." The stranger's face was deadly serious. "Now there is a *bodhisattva* for you, not that he is hiding very much."

"The Dalai Lama sent you to work with Mother Teresa?" the tourist was doubtful.

"Yes, he was very specific. He said, don't just talk about compassion; embody it. So, I went to Calcutta. I had contacts via the Jesuits here"

"Are you a Buddhist?"

"No, I'm just a beggar. Can't afford labels anymore."

"So why obey the Dalai Lama?"

"I just listened to him. That's all. He has no interest in doing the guru trip. He has so much common sense which as you might know is not that common in our world. Are you a Christian?"

"Sometimes, on my good days," the tourist answered defensively.

"How many of those do you have?" the stranger sounded more amused.

"Not many."

"That's why you need more time here." The stranger laughed out loud and gave his belly another rub.

"I've told you." The tourist was a bit annoyed. "I have had enough time in this mad country."

"Mad? Now who is mad?" the scruffy man laughed and pinched a few pegs from the line. He hung a few bits of clothing as he spoke. "How long have you been a racist?"

"I am not..." the tourist stammered and stopped mid-sentence. "Well," he added sheepishly after a pause, "maybe for a few weeks. Some of these Indians are so infuriating, so class and caste obsessed, so racist, rude and uncaring."

"Are they?" the man sounded surprised. "How do you manage it?"

"Manage what?"

"Not to be rude, infuriating, racist and uncaring."

"Fuck it!" the tourist exploded. So what! I'll deal with it when I get home. In two days' time I will be in Goa. Later on, I'll work out what I can manage."

"Why waste all this time on the inside?" the scruffy man grinned. "Crap beaches in Goa anyway. The train leaves from Ranchi tomorrow. In another day you might be in Calcutta with nothing to lose and nothing to defend. Find out who you are here and now, while you can. How about I buy you a ticket?"

The tourist was lost for words.

The scruffy man in the torn orange t-shirt just would not stop laughing.

31

The Dislocated Dreamer

The dreaming boy was too old to remember where he had come from and too young to worry about where he was going. As far as he knew he was here to stay. In his world the dead were never seen. True enough, he had heard rumours about dying. In his comics the bad Germans and the villainous Japs did most of the dying along with some bad guys on television. It all seemed just like make believe. Great stuff for a dreaming boy keen to do battle as the hero of his own ripping yarns. He could disappear inside his day dreams for hours on end. Just like when he played ninja games with the boy next door. Death was never final. They might throw projectiles and swing wooden swords, taking turns to cry 'arrgh' and fall down but the samurai always won the day. No matter how many times they fell down they always went home for dinner alive and hungry. Death was fun for dreamers.

True enough the loud and scary priest at church mentioned death more often than he mentioned heaven. Heaven was supposedly a good place, if you were lucky enough to get there. Heaven was amazing and perfect and off world but none of the adults looked too happy about going there. The loud and scary priest never looked happy. Obviously, lots of things could go wrong along the way. The loud priest also talked about hell more than he did about heaven. None of the adults looked at all happy about going there either. It wasn't hard to see that it might be better to avoid dying altogether. Hell clearly was to be avoided at all costs and heaven could be deferred more or less indefinitely. Sure, heaven might be good but who wanted to die to get there.

It was all abstract for the dreaming boy. He was too young to worry about sermons, even when the loud priest thundered about hell. He was only in church under sufferance. Life was slow and the days were long. He had lots of day dreams to chase and follow. Sermons were something only the poor adults had to fathom.

Once he had seen an old great uncle staggering around his house coughing and moaning like a child. It was a fearsome sight. The old man was out of his mind and his great aunt looked very worried and upset as she tried to get the old man back into bed. It never occurred to him that he too might get old. Even when they told him later that the old man had died, it never occurred to the boy that he might get so decayed and disintegrated. Old age happened only to old people. But then one fine winter Friday his little brother came down with the flu.

No one was that worried at the time. The dreaming boy's mum was a nurse and his dad helped run the hospital for the navy. They made him go to school but this little brother had the day off.

His little brother could be really annoying. Especially when he came and jumped on him in the morning. They were good at rumbling even though he mostly let his little brother win. He didn't like admitting that his little brother was better co-ordinated than he was. He really was the star of the family and the favourite. His little brother was already more spirited, more gregarious, more determined and more fun than he was. Everyone raved about how bright blue his eyes were and how good looking he was. And it was true. He was one hundred percent the bright star of the family. A blue-eyed Celtic avatar in the making.

When the weekend came around, his brother stayed in bed. The doctor came around and gave some medication. None of the grown-ups looked worried. It was just a bad cold that would take its course. Bed rest was enough.

The next day the doctor came back and told them all there was no reason for concern. His mum still did her amazing Sunday cooking. It was treat night when she made cream puffs and sponge cake. They all stayed up a bit late to watch *Gilligan's Island*. The dreaming boy and his little brother laughed merrily when Gilligan got into trouble like he always did. Gilligan was one of the names the dreaming boy sometimes got called by his mum. He didn't like it when his little brother also called him Gilligan but that Sunday night the sponges and cream puffs were so good he didn't mind at all.

When the dreaming boy woke up next morning his dad had already gone to work but his mum looked a bit worried. To his delight she told him she wanted him to stay home 'just in case'. His little brother was still in bed resting. He might have to look after his little sister who also now had a cold. It didn't sound like much fun. School sounded better but the day muddled on just like any other day. At least he could day dream without getting in trouble with his teacher.

Not long later his mum came in and roused him out of his muddled dreams. She looked grim but calm. She told him to keep watch while she went next door to ring the ambulance. There was something very scary about that word ambulance but before he could ask a question she was gone.

Time is a trickster conjuring motion out of stillness and stillness out of motion. One moment things were normal and the next they were not. His brother seemed okay. Then he asked to be taken to the toilet. The dreaming boy got him up and mostly carried him all the way. His little brother looked groggy and tired but he seemed okay. The dreaming boy got his brother on the seat and made to leave him to it.

It was just a little lurch backwards that caught his eye. There and then his brother stopped breathing. The dreaming boy knew somehow it was final. He could see the moment of departure as clear as day. One moment his brother was there, his face and eyes wide open to this world and in the next he was far, far away. In the most slender of slender moments he had gone. His face was swept of presence and his eyes devoid of light. The dreamer started screaming out loud but his little brother was already looking right past and right through him. The dreamer just knew his little brother was going further and further away. Soon he would disappear entirely. Sheer panic shook the day.

The dreamer was still screaming when the next-door neighbour came vaulting over the fence and pushed him out of the way. Suddenly everything was wrong. The dreaming boy kept on crying while the neighbour did mouth to mouth. Nothing made sense. His mum came running in looking scared. Then the ambulance arrived. The dreaming boy couldn't take it in. There was panic. There was his mum, grim faced, riding in the ambulance. He was left alone with his little sister and the neighbour but all he could see, like something he would always see; was the light falling from his brother's eyes as he took his last breath.

Death was no longer a rumour. Rather it was a ground zero, an awakening; a dislocation deep inside from which there would never be a full recovery. He knew now what he had not known before. That death comes to all. He felt the sheer absence, the vanishing of memory, the rupture of connection that made him feel disembodied and lost. He started to wonder who he really was and where he was really going. He found out that grief demolishes the living. He knew now that flesh was weak and could sag, break and unravel in the blink of an eye.

He knew it even more on the dark winter's day of his little brother's funeral. The loud and scary priest was dressed in black and looked as cold and scary as the day. The dreamer cried and cried like he'd never cried before.

Later his mother got double pneumonia and nearly died. Later his father was un-seamed from the inside out. They blamed themselves and refused absolution. Later the dreaming boy grew up discombobulated by his own mortality. One hard death stare was all it took. It made him get too much religion at an early age. He realized that nature was possessed with a brutal degree of efficiency. There will be no new unless the old dies. Every moment from then on always felt a little bit like a free miracle. The horizon always beckoned. The reaper lingered in his dreams.

The sages and saints spoke of birth and death like doorways into other realms. The dreamer hoped they were right. But then it all depended on which realm you might be headed to. Just to be contrary he made a profession out of preferring heaven over hell even though the discombobulating fact of death remained. He liked reminding people that strangely only the dying did not mourn the dead. Death maybe was just a doorway after all.

Wherever and whatever heaven was, one way or another, you always had to die to get there.

32

The Only Adult

The young fan was a true believer. Spring was in the air and finals were coming. It was worth the wait and the discomfort of camping out for tickets. He was with his tribe. All along the line outside the stadium the fellow devotees were camping. There was a buzz of excitement in the air. People were talking, eating, singing and swapping stories like long lost relatives. They knew who they were. They were all for one and one for all. All other teams were merely mortal. They might have bigger memberships and louder war chants but no other team was more dangerous and more ruthless when their backs were against the wall. No other team strode across the ground like a colossus. No other team had the power to destroy the old guard establishment. They were the mighty fighting Hawks ready to swoop and harry through thick and thin. When they roared, their opponents quailed and blanched. When they took the field lesser men tried and failed to keep fear from their eyes.

For as long as he could remember the young fan went to the footy with his dad religiously. They had done the rounds on bitter winter days. They had visited unfriendly territory barking war chants and cursing umpires from the outer. They had been forged in adversity and blessed by mighty victory.

The spring morning was crisp. Beside him two old blokes ate hot dogs and talked over old games. A little further down some country gents in moleskins and shiny leather boots talked in low voices like old squatters discussing wool prices. Next to them a group of older boys were joking and horsing around. Everywhere people looked pleased with themselves. Some rested in swags and others made camp in tents. The young fan didn't feel alone even though he was camping out for himself and his dad. It was finals time and tickets were worth both the wait and inconvenience.

The young fan knew that a day at the football was not without danger. Besides the emotional drama of losing a game, or worse still, the flat out disappointment of a draw, there were always people in the stands to watch out for. Sometimes the worse fights were off field. Once as a young boy on his dad's shoulders he had watched in horror as four grown men kicked another man senseless. When they told his mum she freaked out and banned them from future games. Her prohibition didn't work. She wasn't a believer. A few weeks later they were back again.

Lately he had not been so regular. Surfing had displaced the old tribalism. He was young and fit and a strong swimmer. As a junior footballer he was nothing more than an also-ran player but in the water he excelled. He had taken his share of beatings and submitted to being flogged and mastered by overwhelming force. Twice he had all but drowned but not even the most agro of old sea dogs could get out the back any quicker than he could. More than that; the ocean had claimed his soul. He was young but a grommet no longer. He had faced down more danger than meat headed footy players twice his age. When it came to a choice between surf and footy; football was always the loser.

Except for finals. And especially because his dad wasn't up to camping outside all night for the tickets. It made the young fan's vigil both an act of faith as well as love. There were big games in the offering. All along the line he could feel the buzz of expectation. Once more glory beckoned. The young fan felt his excitement rising. He was amongst the faithful and the day was bright with omens. It was there for him to see when a bunch of Carlton supporters were swooped by a magpie. The young fan almost clapped. Let the contenders bluster and brawl. They were all bound for hard days ahead. The colosseum called.

It was while he was contemplating triumph that a commotion caught his eye. Just away from the ticket line a group of skin heads had started kicking a man on the ground whilst their sharpie girl-friends clapped and screamed and urged them on. The man had his head in his hands and was pleading for them to stop. The skin heads just kept on kicking while the sharpie girls cawed and crowed.

The young fan looked on gaping. He looked to his right. The squatters were busily chatting. Next to them a large man and woman ate some sandwiches and looked away. To his left the older boys had grown quiet. Further down the line no one seemed to be noticing anything wrong going on at all. None of the adults were bothered or concerned. No one but him.

The young fan could not look away. Surely a nearby adult would intervene. Some well-dressed young men walked right past without turning their heads. No one anywhere seemed bothered at all. No one. He got to his feet with his heart in his mouth. He had been bullied at school. He knew what it was like to be outnumbered. He knew his dad would not have looked the other way. He had taught him to stand up to bullies. "Face them down, son. Keep them guessing. Keep your hands in your pockets and they won't know what to do."

That advice had not always worked but he could hear his dad talking. With his heart firmly in his mouth he walked over to the tent with both hands in his pockets. The skinheads were laying into the man with bovver boots. One of them had a knife and another had a wrench. The young fan felt his heart drop to his guts. He looked certain to get something worse than a flogging.

"Why are you attacking this man?" His question fell flat into thin air.

The skin heads were momentarily caught off guard. The leading head kicker who had a long stringy mullet turned towards the young fan with a vicious leer on his face. The sharpie girls looked up and started cursing.

"Fuck him over Macka! Fuck the little cunt!"

The young fan tried to hide his dismay. He looked around and saw a bit of wood lying on the ground. He could feel the day getting uglier by the second.

"Why are you attacking this man?" he asked again, trying to sound polite. The sharpies and skinheads circled like hyenas. The lead mullet looked him up and down while his leer curled into a snarl of contempt.

"What do you want cunt!"

"Fuck him Macka!" the sharpie girls screeched. "Fuck him right over!"

"Why are you attacking this man?" the young fan was surprised he sounded so calm. He looked back to the ticket line. Everyone else had chosen to look elsewhere.

"I am going to fuck you up cunt!" the lead mullet stepped closer. The girls were screeching loudly.

"Kill him! Fuck him up!"

"That's right cunt! The mullet leaned in. "I am gonna kill you."

The young fan could feel his heart racing deep inside his guts. He pushed his hands deeper into his pockets.

"No trouble," he still managed to sound calm. "Why don't we all just walk away?" He looked back at the piece of wood on the ground trying to calculate if he had time to use it as a weapon.

The girls kept screeching.

"Kill him! Kill him!

The mullet leered. "You've got trouble now cunt. We are going to fuck you up."

The young fan fought down another wave of terror and stepped in close, hands firmly in his pockets. He kept hearing his father's voice. "All bullies are coward's son. Frighten one and you frighten them all." The day was disappearing down the toilet. He took another step closer. He felt he had less than one chance. He made eye contact only with the mullet.

"Sure," he sounded calm. "Sure, you, can hurt me. But you now have trouble. You, you, I am going to hurt badly," he spoke evenly not knowing where his bluff came from. All his force and rage was vacuum packed into just that single word; 'you'. He had no idea what he was going to do only that he hated bullies and he had just enough trouble spare for the mullet. He made sure to look nowhere else. If it was going to end badly it was going to end badly for the mullet as well.

The mullet saw it too. No knife or wrench would be enough protection. He took a step back as the hyenas kept cursing. "Next time!" he hissed, "next time we will get you. We will drop from the trees and make you dead meat."

Suddenly the young fans guts relaxed. He almost laughed out loud. The word 'next' and the threat about jumping out of trees told him his bluff had worked. The bullies had no come back. He kept his hands in his pockets and said nothing.

The mullet and his hyenas and the shrill sharpies stepped away cursing, promising death and grievous bodily harm. The young fan breathed easier. He could feel the adrenalin running through his blood. A strange wild confidence swept through him. He watched as the skin heads spluttered and walk away.

His hands were still deep in his pockets.

33

The Retired God Botherer

"You're not in a good way, are you?" the woman at the party waved her champagne glass dismissively. "How about you tell me something positive." She emptied her glass decisively and eyed him sharply. "All this doom and gloom. You don't get out much, do you?" She smiled thinly, covering her mouth to deflect a champagne charged burp.

The retired God botherer gripped his glass of orange juice tightly. He wished he was elsewhere. He should have known. He always sunk like a stone at parties and consistently had the worst of times. An old friend had invited him to his son's welcome home party. It had been an act of mercy of sorts. Something his friend suggested to break his hermetic monotony. Already a recluse; COVID had reinforced his increasing sense of isolation. It had been a few years since he had walked out of his parish after one Sunday too many and told 'City Hall' he could no longer pretend to be Captain Christ. The gap between rhetoric and reality had snapped him in two.

The woman at the party stood nearly a head taller than the retired God botherer. She had big keen brown eyes, gleaming with inquisitorial intent. She had a lithe, athletic look. She wore her hair in a short bob which accentuated her height. She had long artistic fingers and full sensual lips but a frown lingering around her brow gave her a forbidding edge. Her face was handsome rather than pretty.

Their conversation went south quickly as soon as he mentioned the weather. It got worse after he mentioned climate change. As soon as he segued to the topic of the latest international climate report and the fear things might be even worse her brown eyes glazed over. The God botherer watched her doing a quick assay. Her glazed eyes and tight mouth said it all. He was boring, he was tedious, he was intense and he was uninteresting. They sparred for a bit about how urgent it was. Eventually her irritation broke through. She interrupted him mid-sentence.

"Enough of this fear porn! Why don't you plant a few trees and shut up!" She giggled to soften her rebuke. "God help me all this doom loving robs joy. Don't you think?"

So, he shut up as she downed more champagne. For a bit they kept talking inanely while he shrank and she grew taller. He had never been good with women. Always deeply allured but terrified of rejection. Somehow he always felt completely inadequate in the face of their complexity and depth. Celibacy was his default position. He knew it was all about confidence. The tall woman was yet another example. She had more confidence in her little finger than he had in his whole body. Eventually came the question he always dreaded.

"So, what do you do for a living?"

"I am trying really hard now to do as little as possible," he laughed lamely and felt the elevator drop immediately. "It's quite difficult you know but I'm getting there." He tried his best to not let his smile slip.

"That's a stupid answer to a perfectly good question." The tall woman arched her eyebrows and flicked him a dismissive smile. "How about you start again?" The retired God botherer sipped his orange juice pensively and swayed back a little.

"Okay, I used to cure souls until I realised I couldn't cure my own," he tried to start again even as his smile slipped.

The tall woman took an extravagant sip of her drink and tilted her head sideways. She eyed him like he was some kind of strange curiosity. "So are you some kind of shrink," she asked with more than a hint of disdain.

"More shrunk now days," the retired God botherer confessed and wondered irritably why he was saying so much about himself.

"So, what's up? What do you do now?" the tall woman seemed determined to interrogate his sense of purpose."

"I'm practicing social distance and learning more about the world."

"How's that working out for you?"

"Not so good. Do you read the news?"

"Fuck no! It's all fake and full of shit!" The tall woman was vehement. "Life is too short to waste on gloom. The news minders and editors control us with what we get given." she waved her hands in a sweeping gesture of dismissal.

"I don't agree," the retired God botherer stood his ground deciding that he didn't find the tall woman as attractive as he first thought. "We are all in interesting times. COVID, global warming, war drumming, billionaires pissing on the rest of us and telling us it is raining. Have you checked out the news coming out of Canada? Greece, Turkey, China? And now this code red climate report! My God!"

"I don't believe in God," the tall woman flicked her fringe back to emphasize her point. "God is just an abstraction weak people have invented to compensate for not taking responsibility for their own lives. Shit! The weather is always changing. We humans are very smart. There will be technology, we can terraform the world, we can adapt. Sure, there are losers. There are always losers." The tall woman looked him up and down as she spoke. "Anyway, there are too many of us anyhow. Too many leaners and not enough lifters. Too many free loaders! We need a bit of a clean out. Get rid of excess baggage. And get rid of those doomsters who want to send us back to the Stone Age. You might like to join them and build an ark and sail south past fifty degrees longitude. Have a sunny time in Antarctica."

The tall woman laughed. A short high-pitched giggle. The retired God botherer could spot the ethanol fuelled Dutch courage. He saw the sharp glint in her eye and noticed that as she smiled he found her even less attractive. He stepped back and shifted his stance like a fighter

"I don't agree." He decided to push back. "The weather is where life begins and ends. We are in for it. Four degrees of warming since the industrial revolution began is now baked in. Some say even eight to twelve. That's extinction on a massive scale. We will have a shit show very soon. Water wars, crop failures, mega heat waves, mega storms, pandemics, riots in the supermarkets, run away tipping points. And unlike you I believe in God but I am afraid God is not going to save us."

"Bullshit!" The tall woman seemed to be relishing the argument. "Not even your doomster report says that."

"Have you read it?"

"Have you?"

The retired God botherer gulped and stammered. "No, no, just the summary. It is very technical."

"So it is," the tall woman took another swig of champagne and almost sneered. "It has lots of opinion based on models and models are just models. Just graphs and theories and guilt trips." She waved her glass high in the air to underlie her point.

"You can't just dismiss the science," the retired God botherer could not restrain his own irritation. We have been doing that for too long."

"Science!" the tall woman sneered. "Just say the magic word and pretend there isn't any politics attached. Are you a scientist? Did you do that along with whatever it was you did shrinking souls for a living?

"I was a priest," the retired God botherer admitted defensively

"Well, fuck me!" the tall woman was momentarily off guard. "What variety?"

"Catholic."

"Fuck! The worst kind! Kiddy molesters and cross dressers. Now I can see why you don't get out much."

The retired God botherer looked down at the floor wanting to disappear. He sipped his orange juice pensively. He knew there was a good supply of alcohol and drugs at the party. He avoided the tall woman's gaze feeling a sudden desire to get stoned and drunk out of his mind.

"It was just a past life," he said sadly. "In the end the Vatican and I had less and less in common."

"Well good for you getting out of the priest farm," the tall woman smiled her thin smile and gave him a patronizing tap on the shoulder. "Talk about spruiking theories with no basis in reality. I guess eco love inns are your new religion now. Anyway, why is your imaginary friend refusing to save us? I suppose you might say it's divine tough love."

''Something like that," the retired God bother was still looking sadly at the floor.

The tall woman was already turning her head looking for more interesting company. He saw her shrug and start to move towards a group of women standing nearby.

"Good luck with the social confidence." She threw him another thin smile as she turned.

"It's social distancing" he corrected her flatly.

"Whatever."

The tall woman already had her back to him.

Suddenly the coming climate catastrophe felt remote. All the alienation and all the ignorance and all grief and all the oblivion in the world felt like it was arriving inside him, coming up through the floor boards as he watched how at ease the women were with each other. Dismissed, the retired God botherer slunk to a corner of the room and rationed out the last of his orange juice.

Sure enough he was sinking quicker than a stone again. Left alone in his corner he watched and marvelled at how at ease the women were. They were all talking and laughing and giving each other that knowing eye which only women did. He tried not to look for too long. They were so alive and beguiling and strange and utterly inaccessible. The tall woman was breezy and animated and smiled sweetly like butter wouldn't melt in her mouth.

Disgusted with himself, the retried God botherer made for the front door.

Outside the winter air had a sobering chill. He stumbled and looked up to see a crescent moon. "Well, I've just gone to my last party," he spoke aloud to the distant celestial body. His faith wasn't what it used to be.

"Well, go on make yourself useful," he half prayed and half cursed. "Give us a few free miracles. Make me into a woman who can have anyone she wants. Just for tonight. Tomorrow you can end the world on notice."

He stumbled again and cursed. Clearly his prayer was going astray.

The moon kept her distance.

He flushed out his phone and rang the taxi. "Go on," he prayed, "You shape shifting piece of work!"

The moon shone impassively.

Soon enough a big yellow taxi pulled up the street. "Gidday, mate," the taxi driver greeted him in a flat Australian drawl. "Going somewhere?"

The retired God botherer got in and sighed.

"How far will a hundred bucks take me?"

The taxi driver turned and saw the look in his eye. "About half way from here to nowhere," he laughed.

The retired God botherer took one last glance at the silvered moon beaming back unanswered prayers. He belted up and sighed.

"Drive!"

34

The Kindergarten Teacher

The guest could hardly believe his eyes. He was in love. There was a light shining inside the dark. He saw it on both the old kindergarten teacher's face and her daughter. They held hands as they watched the rotating advent wreath make love to the shadows. It was summer solstice and the juggernaut of Christmas was upon them but the silence held. The evening was giving up its secrets. The lighting of the fourth candle was a revelation. All the guest needed was just a moment of time. Silence and magic did all the rest. One solitary stolen glance was enough to unlock the beauty. It had nothing to do with cosmetics or youth. The guest had been beguiled by that often enough. He had seen many a painted goddess not warranting a second glance. This time he just couldn't get enough. It was solstice. They all held hands praying for some unconquerable light to heal the world. He saw that light softly mirrored in the elderly kindergarten teacher and her daughter's face. It was a still pointed wonder manifesting in a humble little suburban kitchen and he was lucky enough to see it. A shy hidden love big enough to make the world new again.

The guest knew his feeling would not last. Christmas was coming after all. No one ever escaped that juggernaut be they conscientious objector or believer. Either you did it or it did you. The small dancing advent candles seemed to disagree. 'Look,' they said, 'and then look again. The light is always here. You just need a mustards seed's worth of grace to see it.'

So, he looked. Beside him the kindergarten teacher's daughter held his hand. She kept her eyes closed reverently even though she was an atheist. Across the small table the kindergarten teacher smiled as she smelt a late rose from her garden. She was old and slow and heavy but the glow in her eyes was young. She sighed and smiled a big sad happy smile.

"You know," she breathed the rose in deep. "Ullie would really love this." She reached across and gave the tiny wreath another spin. The light was doing strange things to her. The advent wreath had the power to move through time. Memories were on the move in the silence. She could see her husband like the first day she saw him. The day she first saw him in the displaced persons' camp was love at first sight.

She closed her eyes as the memories summoned her. There were always things she did not want to remember. She was barely nineteen when Russian artillery started landing in the street. The worst of the war held off until the end. They all heard the stories. It wasn't just the shrill propaganda; news of atrocities were pouring in. It was all too much to figure why the world had gone mad and was tearing itself down stone by stone. She was young and loved teaching the children. She didn't want to leave but all the women were terrified. They were all on the run. It was lucky for her she was young and strong and could march for days with nothing but cold water in her stomach. She was still on the run from the Russians when she laid eyes on Ullie. He was big and strong and on the run from everyone. He was irresistible. The world was broken and vengeance was abroad but she was in love.

No sooner did they reach the camp the English soldiers took Ullie away for questioning. They were shoddy jailors. Everyone was sick and tired of the war by then. The guards turned a blind eye to their assignations. They didn't stop her each time she walked for miles to his camp with her shoes filled with paper to stop the cold and with bread hidden in her coat. They turned a blind eye when she smuggled in cigarettes. She was inventive and a good talker. The guards took pity on her not that she needed their permission. She and Ullie were refugees and the world was in ruins but when it came to new love they needed no one's permission not even God's.

The advent candles kept dancing and catching her eye. This new land on the far side of the world had been good to them. She and Ullie loved the amazing wide landscape. They liked picnics on the beach on cold days with a clean south wind in their faces. They loved their second chance at life. They loved their daughters. They loved their little house and the new friends they met. They loved their work and all the plenty that came with it. Ullie didn't mind the factory work and she was soon a kindergarten teacher again. Most of all they never stopped loving one another. Even when the dark days came and her youngest daughter crashed down with psychosis. With Ullie by her side in a land of plenty they would get through.

The kindergarten teacher sighed and smiled. Yes, she had seen plenty but nothing like the plenitude she and Ullie had known long ago with second-hand newspapers stuffed in her shoes and only morsels of bread in her pocket.

The guest met her eye over the dancing light. He nodded without understanding. The kindergarten teacher's daughter also spoke, her voice all shaky and slowed by medication.

"Yes Mum, Dad and you always loved advent. I like it too.

Christmas is too noisy and too busy. No one is grateful anymore." She closed her eyes like she was in prayer and opened them again. The guest watched her as she spoke. She too was somehow transfigured in the advent light.

The kindergarten teacher beamed back. She had seen her daughter thrown against the wall in the madness. She and Ullie had tried to be a rock of refuge but nothing they did could stop their daughter's fall into the dark. Nothing had stopped that long descent from vivacious dux of school to medication addled locked ward inmate. The doctors tried and time had burnt out some of the psychosis but without their protection their daughter would not have survived.

The kindergarten teacher's daughter saw the knowing look in her mother's eye. They had passed through the eye of the storm together. What awaited no one knew. But she knew more than most people even the smallest light made a difference to the dark.

"It is okay, Mum," she said with a sad happy smile of her own. Life had seized her roughly but she lived for the simple things now.

"Yeah, being broken has its blessings. Now I know what gratitude is."

The guest was amazed. He was not that broken or that grateful. There were outrages in life; defying belief. Being a priest had not stopped him feeling outraged disbelief. There were hurts that cried out for justice. The silence would not hold. The advent candles would burn low and out. He was as good as any atheist on any given day. It did not seem right that that only way to know real blessing was down.

The kindergarten teacher beamed at both her daughter and her guest. She got up to bring in the tea and marzipan and spiced biscuits. She sat back down and smelt her rose again. The perfume rose up rich and free and plentiful.

"You know," she said after a long pause, "I have had a good life."

She paused and smiled like she was all young and on the run again. She could feel it all arising in her heart. "Yes, body and soul."

The guest and the kindergarten teacher's daughter could not help beaming back. The advent light was all over the kindergarten teacher. Both of them could see it

Body and soul.

35

The Child Killer

Every time the new chaplain came to the protection unit, the child killer watched him closely.

Every time the chaplain had that look, like he had permanently lost his way. He was nowhere near as big as the child killer. He seemed reserved and tentative. The child killer noticed how polite and respectful the chaplain was to everyone. He was even polite to the bored officers. Not that it worked.

The bored officer on duty did nothing to conceal her sneer. She kept both feet on the desk while she gave the chaplain the snide treatment the child killer knew only so well. The new chaplain just smiled back sheepishly before politely continuing with his rounds. The child killer noticed how most of the prisoners simply ignored him. The new chaplain was green and untested. It was obvious that he was nothing like his big boned predecessor who used to come back-slapping his way through the unit. The old chaplain had bantered and blustered with the 'plastic gangsters' like he was some kind of favourite uncle.

The child killer watched with contempt as the plastic gangsters strutted and flexed and gave the new chaplain the cold shoulder. Not one of the 'plastics' would give him the time of day either. The child killer watched the new chaplain flounder around the unit until the standover hitman cornered him with his bullshit stories and crappy jokes. The child killer had no doubt the green new chaplain was being milked for information.

The child killer marvelled when he saw that the new chaplain was even respectful to the Mexican. Everyone hated and avoided the Mexican. There was an aura of danger around him that made all the prisoners wary. It was said he was a Narco drug lord. He had connections. It was clear enough to the child killer that the Mexican preferred to be feared than admired. He hated how the Mexican walked around the unit like he was some sort of godfather. All the plastics made sure to respectfully keep their distance but suddenly the Mexican was on his knees. The child killer could hardly believe his eyes. Was the drug lord praying? How was it that the Mexican had dropped his guard? The Mexican actually looked humble and human. Who was this new chaplain?

The child killer had nothing else to do. Every day in the unit was an interminable bore. The clock was always half frozen. Second by tedious second stretched on ad nauseam. He had just a few routines. The sneery, uppity, officers gave him cleaning to do while never looking him in the eye. Sometimes he worked out. Sometimes they let him out into the caged quadrangle that passed as an exercise yard. Sometimes all he did was just sit in his cell and stare out the door and watch the shadows move across the floor. Hardly ever did anyone speak to him. Even the other monsters kept their distance. The plastics thought they were big and hard but they were not as big and hard as he was. He could snap any one of them like a twig. Even the Mexican.

He hated them all, especially the little games they played, strutting and pretending to be hale fellow well met. He hated them all for their hostile faces loaded with judgment. The standover hitman's jokes were all stale repeats. The girly faced serial rapist would not shut up. The Mexican drug lord held court in his cell as if he ran the place. The plastics tried to pretend they were all tourists on holidays. The food was shit. The corrections officers were always sullen and bored senseless. Only the pasty white-collar dude that some other captains of industry had shat down the gurgler sometimes spoke to him. The pasty fallen captain told him how some French philosopher reckoned that hell was other people. It stood to reason. He hated everyone almost as much as he hated himself. If hell was other people then he was in hell and was hell.

The child killer hated the way the daylight hours flayed him with boredom but he hated the nights even more. The worst times were always when he was locked down alone. There were always dreams, haunted by shadows and fears. The blather of the television only increased the dark loathing rage boiling tightly in his chest. He hated all those talking heads and all the smiling, smirking faces. All the on-screen banter filled him with disgust. How dare there be such casual happiness allowed in the world! Didn't they know terror never slept? How dare they all be so cosy and comfortable behind their cheesy smiles and their self-congratulating entitlements. Didn't they know there were hidden horrors in the dark? He raged and churned. He could show them! Yes, he was to be feared, he would wipe all those painted smiles off their faces and make them swap smugness for bitter grief and lamentation.

Every night thin sleep gave little comfort. Sometimes he woke abruptly in cold sweats. Sometimes it seemed he had swum back up to the ordinary dark from some deeper darkness light-years away. Except there never was any light. Somewhere down the lost bones of the world was a place where all light was banished. Beyond that was endless outer dark. He was that darkness. There he was utterly alone save for the demons who never stopped their gleeful accusation. Even the sound of weeping and gnashing of teeth could not drown out their laughter. Every night his demons visited him delighting in the misery of his soul.

Ever since he had been locked up and the key thrown away his demons visited without fail. They made him remember all the faces he wanted so much to forget. Every night he saw the drowning girls he strangled. Every night he saw his co-accused, his 'coey,' dancing his weedy little dance. Every night he saw the same scene again. Every night he saw his scrawny co-accused capering and gibbering with glee. And every morning when he woke and stared at his own reflection he always saw the demon staring right back.

Every night the child killer and his coey were killers on the road again, noon-day devils looking for satisfaction. The two girls never saw them coming. Only an hour earlier he and his coey were just red necked campers. The foolish girls had been hitchhiking. It was his coey's idea to unlock the monster.

"Just a bit of fun," he said. They were smashed out on meth and rushing with adrenalin. The girls had no idea what was coming. As the child killer held them down with his big bare hands, his coey had spun and danced and sang. Every night he saw that rictus snarl of a smile on the weedy evil little prick's face while he whirled like a demented dervish and kept on asking; "Did you see the demon? Did you see the demon?"

Even with all his lust and rage and meth-brained fury, the child killer saw the demon standing there without a shadow to be seen. The sight of his triumphant coey filled the child killer with terror. Every night his coey returned to torment him no matter how many times the child killer destroyed him in his dreams. Each night he was there, giggling and splashing and whooping; wiping away the blood the scratch marks had left on his face. Always he kept giggling the same question, "Did you see it? Did you see the demon?"

As the child killer watched the new chaplain do his rounds, he made up his mind. He went to the officer's desk and made his request. The officers gave him their usual cold disdain and told him to wait while they called the chaplain over. All the while the female officer kept her feet up on the desk as the chaplain approached. "You can see him now if he wants to speak to you," was all she said. She gave both the chaplain and the child killer a look of purposeful contempt, like they were shit on her shoes. The child killer did not know if she was speaking to him or the chaplain. It made him rage inside.

"I need to speak to you alone where no one can hear us." The child killer dispensed with introductions. "I know I'm not one of yours, but it's urgent."

The new chaplain nodded agreeably. "Chaplains are for everybody," he said.

The officers unlocked the gate to the quadrangle and left them to it. They hunched down against the brooding Melbourne winter day and started doing laps. The child killer walked fast saying nothing. It was midday but the child killer could feel all his demons accusing him in the cold air.

He could feel the sharp wind blowing hard against his pounding chest. All his hurt and rage and disgust and fear did laps with him, threatening to blow the dismal sky apart. The silence kept stretching while they made long strides in the short yard.

Eventually the chaplain spoke: "So, you wanted to speak to me?"

The child killer stopped mid-stride and spun about menacingly. "They all say I am as dumb as horseshit," he blurted out like an angry bullied school boy. He walked a bit more and stopped sucking in his breath, drawing on his rage and pain. He found his voice again.

"I don't care who it is. I'll kill all of em! I can kill you!" The child killer leaned in over the chaplain his face a mask of rage and pain. "The fucks! Put me down one more time and I'll snap them clean in two. The next person who wants to shit on me, I am going to kill! It might be one of those dickhead pretend plastic gangsters or that bitch of an officer or some shit head or some smart arse who wants a piece of me, or you!"

The child killer was having difficulty breathing. He glowered and towered over the silent chaplain. Everything was storming inside him. He could see all the plastic gangsters, the sneery officers, his weedy co-accused and those girls whose cries forever echoed in his ear. He could see all the way back down his years. He saw all the put-downs. All the boys at school who called him dumb-ass and all the stuck-up girls who used to snicker behind his back and to his face. All his rage was rising and for the first time in years he was weeping. He was weeping with rage.

"They all want to put me down like a mad dog but I'll kill em! I'll kill em!" The child killer's words tumbled out quickly, raw with intent. He leaned over the chaplain, his body rigid with rage, watching him closely.

The chaplain said nothing. They started doing long strides again. Again they hunched up against the disapproving sky.

Again, they stopped. The child killer loomed in even closer. He held up his thumb and forefinger almost touching. "I have this much of my soul left! This much!" the child killer confessed through gritted teeth; his face contorted with anguish.

"This much!" He could barely breathe as he said it. The child killer thought his heart might stop at any moment. A solitary tear escaped down his face unseen by anyone than the winter sky and the silent chaplain.

"This much!" The gap between the child killer's finger and thumb was closing.

The new chaplain stared back at him and didn't blink. He no longer looked like he had lost his way.

He spoke very slowly, distinctly and softly, "Then you have only one thing you can do now. You will spend the rest of your life atoning and suffering for that last bit of soul."

The new chaplain said no more. A small tear had fallen to the ground. Despite his size the child killer looked shrunken and bowed. He was all out of tears. He gave the chaplain a hard unreadable look and then started walking again. The sky remained unmoved.

There was still space between his thumb and forefinger.

36

The Surprise Guru

It was not love at first sight. She was rough and ready and from the wrong side of town. He was aloof and self-important and had a day job that required lots of pontificating. She was earthy and uneducated. He was a minister of religion and considered himself a sophisticate. He thought she was plain and boring and beneath his level. She thought he was stuck up and out of touch with reality. He had titles and degrees and had travelled widely. She had not been out of the state and her only qualification was being street wise. They had virtually nothing to talk about. The minister was not at all happy that his elderly mother had chosen to employ her as her full-time carer.

To make matters worse she wasn't interested in his work. She did not read and had never gone to church. It did not occur to her that God required middlemen. She thought the word God was just a silly three letter word without a body to it. She thought it better to make optimal use of the present and refused to live anywhere else. When it came to being direct she was not backwards in coming forward. He could talk a good game but she was the one who knew how to be fully Zen with eyes wide open. He thought he was a man of substance. She knew he was liable to blow away when the weather got rough.

She knew a lot about rough beginnings and rough weather. She had been schooled by hard knocks. Her father was an abusive philanderer who cleared off at birth. Her abusive mother preferred sex work and drugs to hands on parenting. Very early on she found herself on the streets. She got to be astute and savvy and street fighter tough. She did not waste time looking back. Instead she got focused on what she wanted. She got good at giving people the sniff test. Despite being dealt shonky cards she developed a knack for drawing out the best in people. Or at least those she liked. If she liked you she usually wanted to love you. If she didn't, then you knew all about it. All the same she made friends easily. It was one of her remarkable gifts. She didn't mind being unpredictable. She could be tender and cantankerous, feisty and moody. She was a good judge of character. Some fools she suffered, others she sent packing. Street life had taught her how to make critical assessments, how to be detached and how to hustle hard if the occasion required. It was quite a wonder she fell in love with such a snob.

Getting the gig as full-time carer was just one of those rare chances in life. The elderly lady lived in a beautiful house by the sea. They met by chance out walking. They got along like a house on fire. They talked, they listened, and they sat just watching the sea. The elderly lady was falling in love. No one had given her so much attention for ages. Certainly not her son.

She also ended up telling the elderly lady a lot of her story. About the abuse, about running away, getting off welfare, coming to the city, working here and working there. Lately, believe it or not, she was working in the security business. She had a few hooks ups but was on her own. It was a fateful day. She got the new gig straight away.

It did not please the elderly lady's son. At first he was quite rude. Not to be put off, she made an effort to have a conversation. When she got to discussing her keen love of ball games he snorted about all sport being a credulous distraction for knuckle dragging Neanderthals. Then she barked something back that made him fall about laughing. That was when she fell in love with him. She was good at reading hearts and she could see something silly and wonderful behind his armour of self-importance.

He started seeing something different about her too. It wasn't her appearance. He thought she was too stocky and drab and her face was not very symmetrical. In a certain light she looked severe; hostile even. And in other lights she looked strangely irresistible. She didn't care about fashion. She kept her hair short with a badly maintained fringe that he found quite unbecoming.

But there were things about her he found amazing. Unlike himself she did not worry about money. Unlike him she did not hanker for achievement and influence. She was not so self-conscious or so serious. He did all the God talking but she was the grounded one. He loved her simplicity and the easy way she could make him laugh. They began taking long walks on the beach and spending more time with each other.

Sometimes when he started to lament the rising tide of secularity and the decline in moral decency she would keep her silence and listen carefully. Other times she just snorted and walked off. She knew it would blow over. She was good with the jokes if he got too intense. She loved seeing him laugh and bringing out his inner fool. She made it clear that life was for the living. She loved walks, good food, kicking back in the sun and doing as little as possible when she could get away with it. She especially loved living by the sea and getting out into nature as often as possible. She felt no need to share his faith.

She only ever liked going to church was when there were no people. There was something about the empty space that made her light headed. She wasn't very used to it. Sometimes she would caper around and do a jig. At first he wasn't impressed. He lectured her sternly about reverence and propriety. She just kept dancing. Sooner or later he would start to laugh and forget what he was talking about.

The more they met the more they both looked forward to it. He loved her embrace and the warmth of her smile. Even more he loved her for her resilience, strength of character and the simplicity of her heart. She just loved him for who he was.

After the elderly lady died, they moved in together. They grew more and more in love. Life was good for a while.

But she knew there would be other rough cards in the joker's pack. She never forgot how she had been abandoned. She knew life was good but it was capricious and cruel as well. She wasn't surprised when they found her cancer. As much as she could, she kept on doing what she loved. She knew there was a price to pay and that every life was owed a death. She knew deep in her bones; grief was the price you paid for love.

As the days wore on he knew who was light weight was and who was heavy. He might possess the titles and do the fast talking but she was the one without pretension. She knew how fragile and threadbare the weave is. He spent so much time arguing, bargaining, denying, refusing and deflecting. She didn't waste time getting to acceptance. She wanted him to know that love was all that matters and that it was the only sane thing in an insane world.

As the end drew near she grew calm and still. She was not one for prefabricated pieties. On the very last day before she died she took a little sip of water from the Buddha bowl and closed her eyes. She drank the clear sweet water before his eyes, savouring every drop just like the Buddha himself. She was gone a moment later.

He could only look on undone and amazed. From day one there was no doubt who the true master was.

She was not only his beloved dog; but his guru as well.

37

The Recalcitrant Priest

When the icon of the blessed Trinity took a sharp turn to the right, the priest knew something was wrong. His chair shook and the revolving bookcase beside him wobbled erratically. Suddenly his little cottage was creaking and groaning like a ship at sea. The crystal ball hanging behind him swung and banged against the window sending great arcs of rainbow light flying across the room. He opened his eyes. He was used to his meditations crashing into distraction but this was different. This time all his inner turbulence was well matched. The rainbow light danced wildly on the walls and his body felt spongy and dislocated. Maybe he was having a turn? Was it an impending stroke or heart attack? His head swung from side to side following the light. Maybe this was it. The light was coming for him or was it just a compressed world finally breaking out in protest.

The unhinged icon commanded his eye. Was his silent God trying to say something? He felt oddly dazed and dizzy. Suddenly the world was no longer solid. Time was stuck. Time was protesting the future. Something was blowing all its circuits. It took ages before he realised he was being struck by an earthquake. Such tectonic events never occurred in his world. The world itself had stopped being solid ages ago. Corona virus had riven the social fabric. Lockdown paralysis had given way to fear and loathing on the streets. For days now, angry, raw, young men had been wrapping themselves in flags and looking for someone to blame. The old securities were going. The old freedoms were being revised. A world of rage, grief and polarity was slouching out of the shambles of pandemic and crisis. War drums were beating. The politics of punishment and blame was outshouting everything else. Finally it seemed, the earth itself had decided to protest.

He knew he had a lot to answer for. He had taken leave from ministry and burnt his bridges with the Church. The old wine had turned to vinegar. His sins and his heterodoxy had taken him down hairy handed paths. Eventually, after a life of speaking too much he had fallen into silence. The gap between rhetoric and reality had grown too wide to cover over. He was redundant to purpose now. An old man watching for death in the snipers valley and held to ransom by regrets. The building continued to rock and his head swayed like a drunk. It would not be so much of a surprise to find he was at the epicentre of some new kind of collapse.

He took another startled look at the right leaning icon of the Trinity. Stray thoughts clambered. What if God really backed the status quo and the ruling order? Maybe he really did have a thing for mega churches, snake oil preachers and even oilier politicians. Maybe God dismissed Jesus, preferring justice over mercy and the big end of town. He knew it all depended on whose God you went looking for. The big end God and the powers and principalities had no need for beatitudes. Blessed always were the rich and privileged. If the meek kept expecting the earth for their heritage that was their problem.

The priest had grown accustomed to being a mass of contradiction. Equal part believer and unbeliever. Equal part puritan and depraved. Once, long ago, he had been an Icarus, a *puer aeternus*, flying towards impossible heights but gravity was a hard task master. It did not take long to crash and burn and find himself bedraggled, bemused and buried in the compromising clay. A lot of gods had called out for his attention since. Sometimes he strived to uphold the faith and at other times he despaired of it altogether. There were days when he played a good Sunday game but he always went home to an empty house. He would watch the last parishioner leave and have to content himself with nothing but the tired pontifications of a disappearing dispensation for company. He had to admit all his gods were constructs. The good, the bad and the ugly. They all knew how to answer back in their own fashion. They bossed and prevaricated and prognosticated like a lot of noisy preachers. His only recourse was to run towards silent obscurity and the unknowing dark. Even there he could still hear his argumentative deities. They still made outlandish claims for supremacy but seasoned doubt had made him fey and resistant to signs and wonders. He still loved Jesus but that old Zen saying about killing Buddha on the road made him doubt every God he ever prayed to.

He closed his eyes again and willed himself still. His body was still rocking. The bright rainbow light had given way to the dark. Something was coming unstuck inside him. There was pinprick of light where the rainbow had been. It was so very far away, so distant and yet so impossibly bright. His body felt like some sort of foreign object. 'This is it' he thought. 'This is it'. The centre could no longer hold; death was marching; anarchy was loosed; and he was falling and falling. He could not feel the chair he was in. All was vertigo and darkness.

He opened his eyes again. The rainbow light and his little cottage was gone. There was a warm sun on his cheeks and the sound of distant thunder. A pleasantly cool breeze massaged his face. Nearby a throng of cicadas were singing loud hymns to the silence. It didn't feel like morning anymore. He was standing and there was a white wrought iron table beside him with two glasses of white wine on it. He looked up and saw he was under a huge oak tree whose shade partially deflected the sun light. He opened and shut his eyes again. The whole world around him felt new and untouched. The sun felt warm and the distant thunder rumbled gently. The breeze brushing past his face felt enlivened with the smell of rain. Looking out he saw a line of green hills rising up to a sand stone escarpment. There was no one to be seen.

He looked down and saw he was clothed in a priestly alb and stole. 'Yes,' he thought, 'I really must be dying.' He closed his eyes and opened them again. The thunder had not stopped rumbling. A thought crossed his mind that he was in some sort of waking dream and his body was still lying back on his cottage floor leaving him stranded in some astral realm awaiting judgment?

He looked again and noticed just how bright and new his alb and stole looked. He looked up. The trees in the distance were a shimmering vibrant green and the ochre sand stone cliffs above were almost luminescent. Nothing seemed old or decayed. The canopy of oak leaves above him were the brightest of spring green. It felt like he had come to some a world made new. He let the feeling wash over and sighed with a certain relief. If he was dying, it didn't seem that bad. For a start, he was pleasantly surprised to find he still existed. So far so good. There were no howls of the damned, no frightening demons or angels, no dissolution of self or de-molecularising of his body.

He looked over at the table. Even the wine in the glasses looked colour saturated. The light glistening over the glass made the wine look fresh and cool. He felt a sudden thirst and was just about to reach out to test his new reality when he heard a voice.

"So here you are." It was an old man's voice. The priest swung his head around but saw no one. Something told him he knew the voice. The educated accent and tone was familiar. There was a note of authority that stirred some old memory.

"Jesus!" The priest exclaimed.

His head went swinging. Suddenly he saw a tall man in a black, Benedictine habit standing on the other side of the wrought iron table eyeing him very keenly. The man was gaunt with a close cropped beard, aristocratic high cheekbones and luminous grey eyes. His hands were folded together while he looked the priest slowly up and down.

"No! I'm not!" The old monks tone was stern. "There is no need to take the Lord's name in vain."

The priest thought taking the Lord's name in vain was as good a prayer as any given the circumstances but stopped mid breath. It was the way the old monk was looking so hard at him. It made the priest glare back. His dread mixed with returning memory. Suddenly he had a flash back. "I remember you! I saw you on an afternoon like this. There was thunder and the day was warm. You tried to scare me straight!"

The old monk nodded. There was a hint of a wry smile on his face but the priest saw steel in the old man's eyes. The thunder in the distance sounded closer. The cicadas were upping their tempo. The air felt heavy with the promise of rain. "It didn't work as I recall," the old monk observed dryly. "Your Bishop was quite disappointed I failed to dissuade you from leaving."

The priest couldn't help staring back. "Where are we?"

"We are in a thin place between realms. We are both passing through." The old man kept looking hard at him.

"To face Judgement?"

"Just each other."

The priest still thought he might be dying. The old monk was giving him a look like he could see right to the secret place where soul is knitted to spirit. He looked down at the table and noticed how the wine dazzled in the light. He felt a strange calm contending with his panic. Old conversations were coming back but the wine looked too good to ignore any longer. He swept a glass off the table and held it up to the light. "Perhaps we should have a toast."

"Agreed" the monk raised the other glass and faced the priest squarely. "To truth."

They clinked glasses. The priest and the monk took a long sip. The wine was deliciously smooth, clean and cool in the mouth and warm all the way down. All at once he felt heightened, clear and focused. Wine had never tasted so good. He felt new from his feet all the way up. He felt sharp and relaxed. All fear and dread had gone.

He looked directly into the old man's eyes. "Another toast," the priest said. "To blind beggars in need of a guide."

The monk hesitated, and then nodded with another wry smile. They clinked again. There was a long silence.

"So," it was the priest who broke the silence. "Truth?"

"Love without truth is meaningless sentimentality."

"Truth without love is a demon."

Both men regarded each other silently. The priest could see that the monk had something more he wanted to say.

"So, you have a particular truth for me?"

"You chose not to serve your people."

"I choose to leave the old dispensation. The franchise and the people are not the same"

"You chose dissent over obedience."

"I chose ferment over fossilization."

"You chose error over unity."

"I chose to get it right by getting it wrong."

"Moral relativism is the highway to hell."

"Relativity and relationship is how the universe works."

The old monk sighed heavily and gave the priest a slightly exasperated look. "Heresy is a half-truth, an instrument out of tune, one small frequency rather than the full bandwidth."

"And still 'God writes straight with cooked lines.'"

"Obedience is not about half measures. You either serve the devil or the Lord."

"And perfection is the enemy of the good. Love a better master than fear."

There was another long silence. The thunder was getting closer. Both men looked hard at each other. On impulse the priest took another long sip of wine. He found himself smiling at the old monk. "So what is it to be? Fire insurance and the big battalions or unlimited mercy? The punishing father or the big embrace? Original sin or original blessing?"

"You are quite recalcitrant aren't you?" the old monk said with a hint of a smile. "Still cherry picking the truth. Do that and you either become a craven libertine or a puritanical fanatic?"

"I have been both" the priest admitted. "As a young man I tried so hard to be straight that I got bent. It didn't end well. I call it the twang effect. That's heresy for you. And who are you an exorcist or an inquisitor?"

"I have been both," the monk admitted. "The devil is a liar and a thorny swindler and error causes lots of carnage."

"So did the inquisition. Where does that leave us?"

"In need of deliverance and salvation." The old monks face was grim.

"Deliverance? The priest rubbed his head thoughtfully. Another clap of thunder sounded nearby. Something stirred in his thoughts. There was a world somewhere else where everything didn't feel new and pristine. Somewhere else there was another world, broken and fey where everything without exception would have to pass through the eye of the needle. All the dispensations, all the churches, all religions and all the empires. Even recalcitrant priests, exorcists and inquisitors. Suddenly he realized why he was here. The old monk was dying. There was something the old monk needed from him and he felt completely empty handed. "You have a demon of pride" the priest said on impulse.

The old monk just gave a slight nod but his face tightened with a hint of some deeper pain. "Ah, yes," he mused sadly, "a real kicker. It is so very hard to have no room to be wrong." His face looked wizened with age as he spoke. "And you have a demon of despair. I've seen that demon many times. No room for anything to begin again. Nothing new under the sun. Only blame and death."

Both men put their glasses down and looked at each other for a long time.

"We are both blind beggars in a thin place" the priest eventually said. "So we must bless each other before we leave. We must choose between the punishing father and the big embrace."

"So it seems" the old monk looked unsure of himself for the first time. "Do you feel hopeless and helpless?" the old monk gave the priest a searching look.

"Yes, almost all the time," the priest admitted softly.

"Then feel it, own it. Help me to feel it. I think only a beggar's prayer will save me."

The priest also looked unsure of himself. He didn't feel he had a beggar's prayer to bless himself with but just then a breath of wind touched his face along with a single drop of rain. It felt like a beggar's worth of grace. The thunder was getting closer. The cicadas were harmonizing down towards full silence. The day felt languid and big enough for any possibility.

"I have less than a prayer." He confessed quietly as if to himself.

"Then pray it!" the old monk looked helpless and vulnerable. "I cannot leave here without your blessing."

More rain began falling. The priest felt his mind go blank and his dread returning. He could feel all his failure writ large. And beyond that was a broken fey other world where prayers went missing all the time. Not a single word came.

The old monk looked hard again at the priest. "Just do it!" he commanded. Then he bowed his head with practiced reverence, closed his eyes and grew very still.

Just then the priest thought he got a glimpse of a distant room filled with rainbow light. He tugged his stole reflexively like he was drawing down power. He stood up to formally bless the monk. There was a long silence.

"May you pray the prayer that wants for nothing," the recalcitrant priest said very quietly.

"And may you have the courage to begin anew." The old monk barely whispered his prayer.

The world went silent.

The recalcitrant priest closed his eyes and raised his hands.

The world went dark again.

He opened his eyes and saw the book case still wobbling and rainbow prismed light still roving over the walls. He sat for a long time.

The world became still again.

Then he got up he straightened the icon of the trinity.

He felt empty.

He felt helpless.

He felt uprooted.

"Well then," he said. "So let's begin again."

Author's Note

There is a shy hope and sensibility running through this motley crew of vignettes that is at odds with our dominant, neo-liberal culture. The culture's view is that we are essentially on our own. From this vantage point there is no interdependence or deeper connectivity. Instead we are offered a world view validating predation, ruthless competition and ceaseless exploitation of matter. Such a world is essentially flat and devoid of enchantment. No deeper coherence or integral meaning is required beyond sorting out who is on top in the struggle of the survival of the fittest. The only fates are those which we make ourselves. Mutuality, co-operation and compassion are for losers

Fortunately this dominant world view continues to encounter resistance. The deeper truth is we are not separate. A growing consensus has been arising within science and the humanities demonstrating our integral inter-connectivity. The bi-polarity inherent in the materialist, neo-liberal world view is undermined by the intuition of the arts, the explorations of quantum realms and by the perennial wisdom and experience of mystics of all stripes.

Once, long ago I came to Lake Mungo in outback western New South Wales. It was a very hot early summer's day with a hard, dry northerly scouring up sand and dust. I wandered around dazed by the heat. The sere beauty kept on inviting me further and further into the lunar landscape. Then I saw the tree which features on the cover of this collection of vignettes. The sight of it struck me as utterly improbable. It felt extraordinary that it should exist at all but there it was, seemingly all alone, bent and wizened, defiantly enduring, with its roots tenderly reaching out though the sand for nurture and life. I took my photo and staggered on.

A bit later I came back towards my car and sat in the shade of a small mulga gum. At first it seemed I only had ants and flies for company but then I noticed a pigeon pecking about at my feet. It too was sheltering from the hard sun, intent on its own agenda. There we were, two non-indigenous travellers taking solace in each other's company. Did we belong to that place and that country? No we did not. But we still belonged to that moment of mutuality and presence. After some time I found some food and left water in a small bowl. Then it dawned on me. Nothing is completely alone. Neither the tree nor the bird, nor me.

So there is a beggar's worth of resistance running through these stories, beginning with a silent witness and ending with a whispered prayer. Although they are in the first instance fictional constructs, the vignettes touch obliquely on some events in my life and others. There is a hint of biography here but the deeper thread running through them is a hymn of sorts to the work of stray grace. Despite the ruling world view, the random chaos of woe contending with joy, and all our moments from the most mediocre to the most intense, everything is held and gathered. Everything somehow belongs.

The title Ninety Nine Names is a brazen appropriation of a Sufi idea. The Sufi's being mystically inclined, maintain there are ninety nine divine names. But because they are not encumbered with something as nonnegotiable as an infallible magisterium, they actually do not have a final agreement on a definitive list. The clear point is that there are many more divine names. Ninety nine is just a cipher for no limit. There is always more instead of less. Abundance and relationship is at the heart of the divine imprint rather than atomisation and scarcity.

So here are thirty seven vignettes with more than ninety nine names in them. Each name calls to another. The supposed distance between us is not what it seems. A shy hope endures in each brush stroke of a story that we are held inside a gracious embrace. No matter how sullied or burnt or broken or just plain ordinary our lives can be, we are part of a greater weave of belonging. No thing and no one is an island. We are always just a one degree of separation away from all things arising.

Vincent Jewell
Barwon Downs
October 2022

Vincent Jewell

Vincent Jewell grew up in Australia during the mid-sixties and seventies including some time living with his family in Papua New Guinea. He spent time exploring various eastern spiritual traditions as a younger man. He trained as a librarian and psychiatric nurse before becoming a diocesan catholic priest. He spent many years in parish ministry and some in prison ministry.

He is now a retired "God Botherer" and lives quietly in his little cottage in the foothills of the Otways in western Victoria.

www.ingramcontent.com/pod-product-compliance
Lightning Source LLC
Chambersburg PA
CBHW020319010526
44107CB00054B/1906